REMEMBER

REMEMBER

Vincent A. Orinda

Copyright © 2013 Dr. Vincent A. Orinda
ISBN: 978-9966-1721-2-9

All rights reserved

No part of this publication may be reproduced, distributed, or transmitted in any form or by any means, or stored in any database or retrieval system, without the prior written permission of the author and Sahel Publishing Association.
The author assumes full responsibility for the research, Bible quotations and all content of this book

Published by Sahel Publishing Association,
a subsidiary of Sahel Books Inc.
P.O. Box 18007—00100
Nairobi, Kenya
Tel: +011-254-715-596-106
www.sahelpublishing.net

A Sahel Book
Interior designed by Hellen Wahonya Okello
Cover designed by Peter Omamo
Editor: Sam Okello
Printed in India, UK, U.S.A
Images courtesy of google.com

"Holy, holy, holy is the Lord Almighty; the whole earth is full of His glory" Isaiah 6:3 (NIV).

TABLE OF CONTENTS

Prologue.. 11

Chapter 1
The Lord Our God is Awesome.................................. 17

Chapter 2
Sabbath – A Memoriam of Creation.............................. 23

Chapter 3
The Wonders of Creation....................................... 40

Chapter 4
And Now Go Tell It On The Mountains........................... 47

Chapter 5
Christ Confirmed The Sabbath Day.............................. 53

Chapter 6
The Day Of Worship Changed.................................... 64

Chapter 7
The Law and Grace... 76

Chapter 8
You Are The Apple of God's Eye................................ 94

Chapter 9
You Are Forgiven.. 101

Epilogue.. 108

PROLOGUE

I am a created being. I was born in a village near Lake Victoria, in the Western part of Kenya. The village is called Gendia. For some reason, this village attracted the first Seventh-day Adventist missionaries in 1906 and also attracted the Muslims around the same time. The Muslims settled at the nearby market called Kendu Bay. And not far from Gendia, the Roman Catholic Church also established a foothold at a place called Mawego.

My birth in this village was like any other. My mother, in labor pains, started her journey to Gendia Mission Hospital to seek care during delivery. Unfortunately for her and her newborn, she did not reach the hospital. She delivered on the way to the hospital. What she remembered vividly was a beautiful flower in a nearby bush. The flower, another creation, brought joy to her painful labor and smiles to her face, as she took a glance at her newborn baby. There was little significance in being born at home or on the way to hospital as this was, and still is, the case for most deliveries in our community.

My mother, Maritha Opon, told me that the Lord had told her to name me Jacob, but my father, Philip Orinda, liked the name Vincent better—the name I must admit I preferred. And even though my baptismal name is Jacob, I have not used the name except in my formative years. As a young child, when anyone asked me my name I would answer, "*Nyinga en*—my name is—Sibli Sibli Kongata Nyawich Kongoro Jacob Akoko." A long name indeed. But apart from Jacob and Akoko, which is my middle name, the rest of the name had no meaning. In fact, my grandparents, Paul Mboya and Maritha Mwango, on the paternal side, and Joel Omer and Miriam Amollo, on the maternal side, made the naming even more complicated, calling me by an additional four nicknames. May the Lord forgive me for not using Jacob, because deep inside me I feel like a Jacob whose name was changed to Vincent.

This book is not about me. In fact, I must confess that I have played no part in its writing as it has all been inspired by the Holy Spirit. But since it is a book about creation, I believe the Holy Spirit is the one that has inspired me to say something about my own creation and the events that preceded the writing of the book.

I loved my mother. She was very spiritual. When she prayed, she talked to the Lord as to a friend. Every time I went to visit her at our rural home in Kosele, a few kilometers from Gendia, we would pray and sing together deep into the night, sometimes until 2:00 a.m. It is during one of those interactions with my mother that she told me how I was born. This was a humbling experience. She went on to tell me that the Lord had revealed to her there was something special that was to happen in my life. For a while, and until now, I have wondered what this "special" thing would be. Now I'm convinced that the Lord has spared my life to be used as a vehicle to put down His words about the Sabbath in this book whose title was also given to me by the Holy Spirit.

I say the Lord spared my life because I have suffered two near-death experiences. Each time I asked the Lord to spare me because I believed there was still much to be done to help the poor, the widows and the orphans. But I did not pray for the

Lord to help me write a book. Therefore all praise and glory be to Him.

The two near-death incidents gave me an opportunity to come closer to the Lord. Through both of them, I learnt that the greatest gift the Lord has given us is forgiveness. *There is life in forgiveness and forgiveness is life.* Christ's life, death and resurrection were all about forgiveness of sinful man who needed to be reunited with the Lord after the separation that occurred in the Garden of Eden.

In June 2010, following a long journey from Nairobi, Kenya, to Falls Church, in Northern Virginia, in the United States, I developed chest pain. At first I did not take this seriously. But as it grew worse, I went into the emergency room at Inova Alexandria Hospital. I was surprised at the urgency with which I was attended to. Within less than an hour I had been diagnosed to have blood clots in both lungs—and one lung was already partially collapsed. I had difficulty breathing. I was taken to the Critical Care Unit and was put on oxygen, with close monitoring and injections to take care of the clots. Before going to the Critical Care Unit, I asked the attending doctor a question. "What's my prognosis?"

She said, "Do not worry, if you were to die you would have died already."

I remained on oxygen for 3 days. During this time, I sought the Lord intensely and prayed for forgiveness. I also searched my heart for any wrong anyone may have done to me and told the Lord that I forgave them. After discharge, I was put on blood-thinning drugs to prevent any further clots.

14—Remember

I remained on the blood-thinning drugs until June 1, 2011, when my doctor decided that I no longer needed them and should stop using them after I underwent some tests. At that time, I had done consultancy work for Namibia and was under enormous pressure to finalize and submit the report. I heard a voice telling me that I needed to finalize the report quickly and send it to Namibia because something may happen to me and may be it would be difficult for anyone to find the correct final version. I completed the report on June 1, the same day the doctor cleared me. About fifteen minutes after completing the report, I felt an urgent urge to go to the toilet. Sure enough, I saw red blood in my stool and was immediately alarmed, knowing that I was still on blood thinners. I bled a lot.

I told my wife, Ingrid, that I needed to go to the hospital. I did not tell her the extent to which I had bled because she was also not well. She could not drive me to the hospital because a few days earlier, she had undergone surgery for back pain, arising from a slipped disc. I had to drive to the hospital myself. My daughter, Miriam, was at home and accompanied me to the hospital. Just before leaving the house, I had a second bout of bleeding. By the grace of God I arrived at the Riverside Hospital, in Newport News, in Virginia. As soon as I arrived, I had a third bout of bleeding. I was taken to the emergency room, examined and blood samples taken. While still on the examination table, my daughter, who was with me in the examination room, heard me say, "Oh my God" then I passed out. She later told me she thought I had died.

When I woke up, I looked at my hands and they were white. I had lost a lot of blood. My blood pressure was very low. I was given four units of plasma within an hour and taken to the

Critical Care Unit again, under oxygen. I told the Lord to save me—that I still had a lot to do for Him. Many people prayed for me. And my children—Peter, Akinyi and Miriam—agonized prayerfully as they came to terms with my second near-death encounter within a period of a year.

While still in the Critical Care Unit, the doctor told me that the plan was to find where I was bleeding from and then he would do surgery to remove that part of the intestine. He said if I'd had another bout of bleeding, my heart would have stopped because of anemia. I was put under "Nil by Mouth," except fluids, awaiting colonoscopy and possible surgery. On the second day in the hospital, there was no bleeding. I received blood transfusion because my hemoglobin level was low after the massive bleeding. On the third day, I had a slight bleeding and was taken for colonoscopy. The doctor was hopeful that he would identify the bleeding site after which I would go to theatre. But the Creator had other ideas. He performed a miracle. The doctor looked everywhere as he examined my intestines. He could not see any spot where the blood had come from. I felt strongly that the Lord would heal me. I was later moved to the general ward.

It was now the fourth day, a Sabbath day. I left stronger and continued to pray. I enjoyed messages from my Bible. In the middle of it all, I heard a voice telling me to go home because I was healed. I told the doctor I was going home. He could not keep me because there was no longer any bleeding. I was healed. The blood-thinning drugs had also been stopped.

Looking back at the two incidents, I have no doubt in my mind that the Lord saved me to tell the world about the Sabbath.

Because of His miraculous healing, I can do no less than proclaim it from the shores of the Victoria to the top of the Empire State Building, and from the valleys of the Rio Grande to the undulating, jugged tips of the Alps that the Creator of the wonders we see around us has asked man to do one simple task—REMEMBER. This book examines the fourth of the Ten Commandments. I pray that the Holy Spirit will lead you as you read this book and learn to celebrate God's creation as was originally intended.

CHAPTER 1

THE LORD OUR GOD IS AWESOME

The Stage Is Set

We are reminded and called to accept our nothingness

This book is about creation. It's about giving glory and honor to the Lord God our Creator. The book takes us back to the origins of the earth and the entire universe. It brings to the fore God's revealed words and commandments to mankind, and about the joy He had after creating everything by the spoken Word and with His hands.

It is evident that the heavens, the earth and the entire universe are a testimony to God's greatness. Yes, our God, the God of Abraham, Isaac and Jacob is awesome.

As it is written in the book of Acts 17:24-25:

> ***Vs.24*** The God who made the world and everything in it is the Lord of heaven and earth and does not live in temples built by hands.
> ***Vs.25*** And He is not served by human hands as if He needed anything, because He himself gives all life and breath and everything else.

Now, the reason this book opens with God's confounding questions to Job during his trials and temptations is simple—it is because in those questions, God revealed, perhaps more than anywhere else, that He is the awesome creator. What He told

Job came down to this, "Job, I am the creator of the heavens and the earth, the ruler of everything. I know what goes on everywhere, anytime; and I direct all events as I please, for I am the Lord God of the universe!"

Job was a faithful servant of God, who lived his life only to serve his master. So faithful was he that one day, after the devil had passed by to say *jambo* (hello), that disgruntled, ancient deceiver left Job's presence and went to taunt God. He said, "Wait a minute, do you think Job worships you for nothing? It's the wealth!"

"Then go test him," God said.

What followed was a withering torment that left Job and those around him confounded. But Job never wavered in his love and worship of God.

"Maybe it wasn't the wealth after all," the devil came back to complain. "Maybe it's his good health."

"Then try your luck," God said. "But don't touch my servant's life."

I have paraphrased the discussion between the Lord and the evil one. If you read the account that follows, what you see is what a man who deeply knows the Creator can withstand. Job knew that the Lord, who created the heavens and the earth, controlled events around him however nasty things turned out to be. But you also realize that when things get so dire, the folk around us can be used by forces opposed to God to destroy our faith. In Job's case, so persistent and vociferous was the attack on his faith by his friends and wife that he must have wondered what kind of friends he had.

Because of the relentlessness and his wife's final counsel for him to abuse God so he could die, Job got tempted to ask God a few questions. He wanted to know what God was really up to. Things didn't seem to make any sense.

But God's words in Job 38 are just too powerful to be glossed over. In this opening chapter, I want them to serve as an anchor for the discussion that will follow. What we seek to underscore is not the fear that should grip us for having not recognized God as the Creator that should be worshiped, but our need to take a fresh look at the loving hands that placed us in this world.

Here is the Lord in His own words:

Job Left Speechless

> **Vs1:** Then the Lord spoke to Job out of the storm. He said:
> **Vs2:** Who is this that obscures my plans with word without knowledge?
> **Vs3:** Brace yourself like a man; I will question you and you shall answer me.
> **Vs4:** Where were you when I laid the earth's foundations? Tell me, if you understand.
> **Vs5:** Who marked off its dimensions? Surely you know! Who stretched a measuring line across it?
> **Vs6:** On what were its footings set, or who laid its cornerstone?

Vs7 while the morning stars sang together and all the angels shouted for joy?
Vs8: Who shut up the sea behind doors when it burst forth from the womb, **Vs9** when I made the clouds its garment and wrapped it in thick darkness, **Vs10** when I fixed limits for it and set its doors and bars in place, **Vs11** when I said, "this far you may come and no further; here is where your proud waves halt?"
Vs12: Have you ever given orders to the morning, or shown the dawn its place, **Vs13** that it might take earth by the edges and shake the wicked out of it?
Vs16: Have you journeyed to the springs of the sea or walked in the recesses of the deep?
Vs17: Have the gates of death been shown to you? Have you seen the gates of the deepest darkness?
Vs18: Have you comprehended the vast expanses of the earth?
Vs19: What is the way to the abode of light? And where does darkness reside?
Vs22: Have you entered the storehouses of the snow or seen the storehouses of the hail?
Vs24: What is the way to the place where the lightning is dispersed, or the place where the east winds are scattered over the earth?
Vs25: Who cuts the channel for the torrents of rain, and paths for the thunderstorm, **Vs26** to water land where no one lives, an uninhabited desert, **Vs27** to satisfy a desolate wasteland and make it sprout with grass?
Vs28: Does the rain have a father? Who fathers the drops of dew?

Vs29: From whose womb comes the ice? Who gives birth to frost from the heavens?
Vs33: Do you know the laws of the heavens? Can you set up God's dominion over the earth?
Vs37: Who has the wisdom to count the clouds?

And there's more in Chapter 39

Vs1: Do you know when the mountain goats give birth? Do you watch when the doe bears her fawn?
Vs5: Who let the wild donkeys go free?
Vs19: Do you give the horse its strength or clothe its neck with a flowing mane?
Vs26: Does the hawk take flight by your wisdom and spread its wings towards the south?
Vs27: Does the eagle soar at your command and build its nest on high?

These were troubling questions that left job speechless. The Lord seems to have been asking Job this—do you really know me as your Creator and Sustainer? Do you know I knew you before you were formed in your mother's womb? Why have you not paid attention to my created works?

In the coming chapters of this book, we are going to look at a single word God pronounced. The word carries more weight than a world reeling and rocking under the weight of the devil's sustained lies has cared to realize. But because of the gravity of the word REMEMBER—in relation to matters of creation and eternity, and because of the imminent return of Christ—this book takes the view that the time to tell the truth is now or forever hold your peace.

After the withering, pointed questions the Lord asked Job, the confounded man finally answered in Job 40:4:

> *I am unworthy—how can I reply to you? I put my hand over my mouth.*

To those penetrating words of Job, there is nothing to add. Suffice it to say that after reading this book, everyone should search their hearts and answer the question: "Why did God ask mankind to remember His Sabbath?"

CHAPTER 2

SABBATH – A MEMORIAM OF CREATION

In the beginning God created the heavens and the earth (Genesis 1:1). The earth was formless and empty. There was no universe and no light. There were no plants, animals, insects, fish, birds, water, grass, the air we breathe and no man or woman. But God the Father, the Son and the Holy Spirit were there. After God created everything in five days, there was one more day left of creative work. That's when God said, "Let us make man in our image, in our likeness, and let them rule over the fish of the sea and the birds of the air, over the livestock, over all the earth, and over all the creatures that move along the ground." *Let us*—the Father, the Son and the Holy Spirit spoke. This was a selfless act of love. Thus the Lord formed man from dust of the ground and breathed into his nostrils the breath of life and man became a living being (Genesis 2:7).

In Genesis 1:31, it is written, "God saw all that he had made, and it was very good. And there was evening and there was morning—the sixth day."

By the sixth day God had finished the work He had been doing, so on the seventh day He rested from all His work (Genesis 2:2). And God blessed the seventh day and made it holy, because on it He rested from all the work of creation that He had done (Genesis 2:3).

Creation was the result of love. God looked back at His creation and the exciting six days in which all the work was done and declared that there must be a day in man's life when man celebrates creation. That day is the Sabbath day. So God commanded us to REMEMBER the Sabbath day and keep it holy. God put this very clearly in the 4th Commandment. It reads as follows:

> *Remember the Sabbath day by keeping it holy, six days you shall labor and do all your work, but the seventh day is a Sabbath to the Lord your God. On it you shall not do any work, neither you nor your son or daughter, nor your manservant, nor your animals, nor the alien within your gates. For in six days the Lord made the heavens and the earth, the sea, and all that is in them, but he rested on the seventh day. Therefore the Lord blessed the Sabbath and made it holy* (NIV).

The key words are: Sabbath, Remember, Rested and Blessed.

In the text we interact with several ideas. In order to make this a simple read, let me list them as follows:

- The Sabbath day is memorialized for creation.
- It's a day declared by God to be a day of remembrance.
- It's a day to remember that we are created beings—created in His likeness.
- It's a day to remember where we came from.
- It's day to remember that we are just but dust.
- It's a day to totally surrender to Christ to the glory of the Father.
- It's a day of reverence as we come to the Lord in prayer, offering praises unto Him (our Maker and Redeemer).

The fourth commandment has not been accorded its rightful place in the cosmic scheme of things. To be sure we have an understanding of its foundational importance, consider that it is the only commandment—of the ten—that has a bearing on the only lasting covenant God entered with man. The Sabbath day was there from the beginning and will be there into eternity. It was there before anyone lied or committed any sin. It was there when only holiness and purity existed. In other words, the Sabbath covers the span of time from one eternity to the other, as it is written in the book of Isaiah 66:22-23.

I'm sure you are beginning to sense how difficult it is to conceptualize something of the magnitude of the Sabbath in my inability to adequately describe it. One songwriter, in his zeal to crystallize eternity, used several words that he later decided were not…right. Finally giving up, he merely said,

"And forever is a long, long time!" Do you get it? That is what the Sabbath is. To understand its significance, you have to understand the Creator.

Here is a glimpse of Him. He is:

- Source of life
- Source of help
- Source of strength
- Source of power
- Source of light
- Source of salvation
- Our hope and redeemer

If this is not an amazing portrait of God, what is? He is everything! No wonder fallible theologians and dumbfounded philosophers coined the three terms to describe His person as omnipotent, omniscient and omnipresent. He alone is worthy to be praised. And because of His enduring love for man, the Sabbath day should always reflect the good God intended man to find in it. It should be:

- A day for celebration
- A day of joy
- A day of promise
- A day of honor
- A day to devote ourselves to our Father, the Almighty God

- A day to accept and acknowledge Christ as Lord and Savior
- A day to seek the presence of the Holy Spirit
- A day to think of no one else but God
- A day of praise
- A day to pray without ceasing as we worship God
- A day of blessings
- A day to renew our vows to the Lord
- A day to remember that God cares
- A day to give up our will and allow God's will to take over and lead us according to His purposes
- A day to focus on Christ as our savior

- A day to spend time with God and remember that the time we live in was created to be cherished and not to be wasted in ungodly things
- A day the Lord blessed and made holy because on it He rested from all the work of creation He had done (Genesis 2:2)

It Was Very Good

Most of us dive into the Sabbath without stopping to comprehend the creative work that preceded it. It is critical that we see the 7-day week as an integral part of God's planned rest on the seventh day. In other words, the rest that we must have on the seventh day cannot be divorced from what man has to do the other six days of the week. The Lord did what was good through the week, then rested on the Sabbath. In similar fashion we, who are His created beings, should emulate our Creator and do good during the week. It does not comply with God's desire for man that we should fight, quarrel, gossip and harm others during the week, then reserve the Sabbath as an isolated day to do good. The Sabbath day is a call for us to be in a permanent state of experiencing Sabbath rest all the days of our life. Are we together?

So on the Sabbath, as God looked back on His creation, with a smile on His face, He sat back, rested from all His work and declared an everlasting memorial. *The Sabbath.* God could have gone on to create more wonderful things, but He looked at what He had made and declared it very good. And very good for God is more than man's excellent. Man cannot understand this level of goodness.

But that's not what this matter is about. The beauty was great for sure. And God's pronouncements were timely indeed. But it is what God did not ask of man that is of critical importance here. Notice that God did not ask man to *know exactly* how He formed him and how He worked through the complicated connections in the human body. He did not ask man to *study* how He made him breathe spontaneously in his sleep and how man's heart would beat for years and years. And neither did He ask man to *comprehend* how his ears and eyes and brain and hands and feet worked in coordinated harmony. No, He didn't command man to *figure out* how the kidneys filtered unwanted elements, the stomach digested food, and blood carried oxygen to all parts of the body. This would have been too much for man. God simply said REMEMBER me as your Creator. And that would be enough. Can you believe this?

Remember Yes, But How?

First of all, God wanted man to remember that he was a created being. Having been created, man was to remain beholden to his Creator and worship Him. That was the reason God blessed the Sabbath—the seventh day since He started the creation of the "heavens and the earth and the sea and all that is in them"—and made it holy. God thus commanded the man He had made to "Remember the Sabbath day and keep it holy." That didn't seem like much, did it?

And to stress the importance of the Sabbath (the fourth commandment), He personally handed it down to man, through Moses, among the Ten Commandments. This act of handing the Ten Commandments was a way God revealed Himself to the children of Israel. It was God's way of telling the Israelites that His nature would never change—just as the engraved statutes of the commandments would last forever. Later, in Christ, God revealed Himself further and even continued to demonstrate the everlasting nature of Sabbath rest as He lay in His grave.

But as Ephesians 6:12 (NKJV) points out, we do not wrestle against flesh and blood, but against principalities, against powers, against rulers of the darkness of this age; against spiritual hosts of wickedness in the heavenly places. This was God's way of warning that it would never be easy to keep the Sabbath holy. It was going to be a struggle. Today, as we look at the manner principalities have dealt ruthlessly with the Bible and the Sabbath, it is easy to see why Christ was concerned. The Bible has been banned, burnt, desecrated, humiliated and even jeered in sections of the world, but it has never failed to torch off fires that led its tormentors to later wonder about their actions. It is not farfetched to imagine that such tormentors met the Sabbath in the Bible once they settled down to read the book.

It Would Never Be Easy

To the weary, Christ had this to say, in John 7:37-39:

- Let anyone who is thirsty come to me and drink (Vs 37).
- Whoever believes in me, as scripture has said, rivers of living water will flow from within them (Vs 38). By this He meant the Spirit, whom those who believed in Him were later to receive. Up to that time the Spirit had not

been given, since Jesus had not yet been glorified (Vs 39).

From the foregoing, you realize Christ was aware the going would never be easy. So concerned was He about the future travails of His followers that in one of His far-reaching pronouncements in Matthew 11:28-30 He said:

- Come to me all you who are weary and burdened, and I will give you rest (Vs 28).
- Take my yoke upon you and learn from me for I am gentle and humble in heart and you will find rest for your souls (Vs 29).
- For my yoke is easy and my burden is light (Vs 30).

This matter of His light burden has been problematic to folk around the world who have wondered about the catastrophes prevalent in the world today. Though a comprehensive, exegetical look at His words in this passage is beyond the scope of this book, I will make a brief comment later on the text. For now, may it suffice to say that whoever enters a Sabbath rest—as opposed to rest on the Sabbath day—will surely come to that point where he/she can say, "The Lord's burden is light!"

Spending The Sabbath With God

Matthew 12:12 says, "Therefore it is lawful to do good on the Sabbath." Based on this text, many people have gone out to do what they perceive as good. They do this to please God. In and of itself, pleasing God is not a bad thing, but it is not what Christ is talking about in the text. The son of God is asking us to get out there and touch other people's lives in a way that reflects His glory and character to them. He wants us to engage in actions that grow our commitment to Him and enlarge His kingdom. Let me list below what the Sabbath is in terms of expected behavior:

- A day to visit the sick and pray for them
- A day to give to the poor, the widows, and the orphans. *For whoever is kind to the poor lends to the Lord and He will reward them for what they have done* (Proverbs 19:17)
- A day to humble oneself before the Lord of the Sabbath to the glory of the Father
- A day to cast a net for Jesus Christ
- A day to remember Jesus' words: Father as you sent me, so I send them
- A day to marvel at the works of the Lord
- A day to look at the trees, the grass, the birds, the animals, the earth, the seas, the stars, and the heavens
- A day to taste God's goodness with greater passion as we look at God's creative power. For it is written, *Taste and see that the Lord is good; blessed is the man who takes refuge in Him* (Psalms 43:8)
- A day to dig deeper and renew the weekly search for your purpose in life, as you think about creation and that part you—as a created being—was created to do
- A day to enjoy the hope of the second coming of our Lord Jesus Christ
- A day to remember that we are but dust—God's breathe of life. This means that apart from God we are nothing. And this is why God wants us to be humble, not haughty and arrogant. So once a week, on a Sabbath, let us fall at the foot of the cross, humble

ourselves before God and surrender all. We must be keen to the fact that all we are and all we have belong to the Lord our God

It is difficult to appreciate the creative power of God if your senses are not in tune with the beauty around you. To try to awaken that sense, let me create a scenario for you. It is Sabbath morning in Hampton, Virginia, at 8:00 a.m. I'm sitting near the kitchen window with the sun directly in front. The clouds are forming and changing patterns, with a deep blue sky behind. The sun rays are penetrating the sky and smiling on the trees, which stand tall with no leaves; just buds waiting to bloom. The grass looks weather-beaten, but is beautiful still. Yes, it is still winter, but it will soon be over. Do you feel it? Sense it? Love it? God created such beauty around us then asked of us just one thing: REMEMBER!

The Lord is calling upon each of us to remember that He, the God of Israel, the God of Abraham, Isaac and Jacob, He created us in the most unselfish manner (Genesis 1:26). His unselfishness is reflected in these words: "Let us create man in our own image, in our likeness, and let him rule over the fish of the sea, and the birds of the air, over the livestock, over all the earth, and over all the creatures that move along the ground."

Do you see how selfless God acted? It amazes me just to imagine that a God so vast in power would worry about fairness, justice and above all love for *me!*

But what must fill us with awe—if nothing else ever will—is the fact that the Lord knows us well. There is nothing we can do that catches Him off-guard. Let me walk you through the relevant verses of Psalms Number 139 so you get a sense of just how intimate the Lord knows each of us:

- ***Verse 2:*** You know when I sit and when I stand; you perceive my thoughts from afar.
- ***Verse 3:*** You discern my going out and my lying down; you are familiar with all my ways.
- ***Verse 4:*** Before a word is on my tongue you know it completely.
- ***Verse 13:*** For you created my inmost reins; you knit me together in my mother's womb.
- ***Verse 14:*** I praise you because I am fearfully and wonderfully made; your works are wonderful, I know that full well."

I don't know about you, but for me, the very fact that my God knows me so intimately is pretty sobering. This is God's way of telling us that He is watching how we represent Him in this world. He expects us to handle one another and the environment with care because He has placed us here as stewards of all that He created. But in the event that we fail to live up to His expectations, He has promised forgiveness and a brand new start—not once, not twice, but each time we falter and come to Him to wash away our sins. In this regard, the Sabbath was also created to remind us of the forgiveness the Lord extends to us when we:

- Worry all the time as if He is not there for us
- Have anxiety that paralyses us as we try to rely on our own strength
- Have fear

- Give up
- Blame others for the things happening in our lives which we do not like
- Refuse to love our neighbors
- Are upset all the time
- Say " I cannot do it" or "I am unable" or "I am worthless"
- Refuse to acknowledge God
- Call what we get "luck"
- Are boastful of achievements in our lives
- When we forget what is written in Colossians 3:17, which says, "And whatever you do, whether in word or deed, do it all in the name of the Lord Jesus giving thanks to God the Father through Him."
- Refuse to see God's blessings in our lives
- Have doubts as to whether or not our prayers will be answered
- Not able to forgive even as we ask for forgiveness
- Fail to love as the Lord loved us

Once every week the Lord has asked us to REMEMBER. As we do so we are drawn closer to Him. And yes, we must seek the Lord and glorify Him daily and love His creation as we prepare for the weekly dedication and remembrance of the Sabbath day. This seven-day cycle of rest every Sabbath was the Lord's way of reminding man of the need for a break in the hectic pace of daily life so that man could reflect on matters of greater importance. God certainly knew what man needed. This critical break (Sabbath rest) was His way of saying, "Remember thy Creator!"

One People

The Sabbath must also remind us that we are one—a people created in the likeness of God. One in Christ. When we look at any human being on the face of this earth, we should stop seeing a tribe, race, color or creed. We should stop seeing a social class in which we belong.

We are all created in the image of God. In His likeness He has created us. So when we hate anyone we are saying to God "I hate you." If these are not inappropriate words to tell the Creator then which ones are? Jesus must have had this in mind, in His Sermon on the Mount (Mathew 5), when He said:

> **Vs21:** You have heard that it was said to the people long ago "You shall not murder and anyone who murders will be subject to judgment".
> **Vs22:** "But I tell you that anyone who is angry with a brother or a sister will be subject to judgment. Again anyone who says to a brother or a sister "Raca" is answerable to the court. And anyone who says, "You fool!" will be in danger of the fire of hell."

God makes no junk. God hates no one. He loves sinners and good people alike. So He calls on man, created in His image, to love as He loves. But this can't be easy for fallen man, can it? That's why Christ felt the need to stress the point in Mathew 5:44-45:

> **Vs.44:** "But I tell you, love your enemies and pray for those who persecute you,

Vs45: "That you may be children of your Father in heaven."

After that powerful reminder from the Lord himself, I don't wish to say much more, except to be candid in interpreting those words into our context. What Christ said was this—*Love everyone the Lord created...pray for them and embrace them, even the enemies.* That is what it means to enter the Sabbath of eternal rest. *And let me add that if you or I show love and kindness to a child we do not know and who "does not look like us," we put a smile on God's face!*

Thus The Sabbath Was Made For Man

In concluding this chapter, it's important to recognize that the Sabbath belongs to God and not to man. It does not belong to any religion. And it certainly does not belong to the Jewish people as is often mentioned by those who refuse to acknowledge the centrality of the fourth commandment. The Sabbath belongs to the Lord, who established it at creation, long before the Ten Commandments were passed on to Moses and before any religion had emerged.

Jesus put it best, when one Sabbath, as He and His disciples walked along a grain field and His company picked some grain to eat. He engaged Pharisees who accused them of breaking the Sabbath. The Pharisees said, "They are doing what is unlawful on the Sabbath" (Mark 2:24).

Jesus answered thus, "The Sabbath was made for man and not man for the Sabbath. So the son of man is Lord even of the Sabbath (Mark 2:27-28).

In spite of the complaints from the Pharisees, Jesus continued to heal the sick and care for the needy on the Sabbath day. He met a man with a withered hand in a synagogue and suddenly the same lot of Pharisees complained about the healing He performed. He told the man to stretch his hand and it was restored.

Later, in Jerusalem, Jesus went to a poolside where folks used to wait and jump in when the waters were stirred so they could heal. An invalid who had waited 38 years since no one had ever offered to help him on was asked by Christ if he wanted to be healed. Christ said, "Do you want to get well?"

The man said there was no one to help him get in the pool.

Jesus, moved by the man's situation, knew there was no time for making this a teachable moment; He simply said what needed to be said then. "Pick up your mat and walk." The man was cured instantly—and it was a Sabbath!

Now, notice something strange here. Instead of the Pharisees thanking God for the miracle of healing, they said, "It is the Sabbath; the law forbids you to carry your mat." The legalistic Pharisees were more concerned about keeping the Sabbath than the plight of the sick. They thought the Sabbath belonged to them. But in performing these miracles on the Sabbath Christ was passing a message that the Sabbath was made for man, not man for the Sabbath. It was created so that man could give glory and honor to God.

As Jesus did, we should do good on the Sabbath. But we must be careful to observe the Sabbath according to God's commandments and not engage in any activity for private gain. We can go out to pray for and comfort the sick; we can reach out to the widows, the hungry and the orphans; we can even go out to share the Word and bring people to Christ, but deep down we have to remember that Christ is the Lord of the Sabbath!

CHAPTER 3

THE WONDERS OF CREATION

The Bigger Picture

The awesomeness of the Lord our God is beyond man's comprehension. We have a glimpse of God's greatness and awesomeness when we take a closer look at His creation. And as we do so, let us take a moment to think about the wonders of His handiwork. We are in the universe, flying with great speed unknowingly as we go about our day-to-day events and occurrences. We are mostly unaware that the universe, which we are part of, is a massive creation that stands out and represents the greatness of the Lord our God.

The Milky Way

In the universe is the Milky Way—the vast Galaxy that contains the Solar System. Before the time of Galileo Galilei, the Milky Way was seen as just a band of light. It was an impressive array of stars that meant nothing except, perhaps, to sailors and other students of the starry formations. That changed in the year 1610 when Galileo used his powerful telescope to discover that the Milky Way was not just a band of light, but was in fact made up of individual stars. This was an astonishing discovery. Then in 1920, Astrologer Edwin Hubble further identified the Milky Way as just one of about 200 billion galaxies. Did you get that? I said 200 billion! The Milky Way was just one among the 200 billion galaxies, but in its case, it was found to have between 200 and 400 billion stars. Let me repeat 400 billion—and remember we are talking about God and the wonders of His amazing creation.

Now listen to this one. Our Solar System—with the nine planets that orbit the Sun—is within the Milky Way and is just one of the solar systems. There are others. And the Milky Way Galaxy contains many planets, 10 billion of which are located in the habitable zone of their parent star. The galaxy that neighbors our Milky Way galaxy is called the Andromeda Galaxy which is believed to have one billion stars, at least twice the number of stars in our Milky Way Galaxy. All this information, and the ones below, are readily available in *Wikipedia* and other relevant references.

Triangulum Galaxy

The third largest galaxy is called Triangulum Galaxy, which has about 10 billion stars. This galaxy can be seen by the naked eye if there are clear skies in the evening. From wherever you are, try locating this creation with your naked eye and just stop for a second to marvel at the God who put it all together. It is humbling that such a God would care to send His son to die for you—and most of all for a sinner of my magnitude.

But we are not done. I know this is staggering stuff, but how else will you understand the greatness of our God if I don't tell you what defines Him as such? Let me keep going. It is believed that the Milky Way is moving at a fast speed of 630 kilometers per second relative to the local co-moving frame of reference. Right now you are moving within the Milky Way at a speed of 630 kilometers per second. Can you imagine that? And at the same time the earth travels at about 51.84 million kms per day. If you are like me—when I first heard of these mind-boggling numbers—you are probably saying, *Who cares?* Well, we all should care. The devil has been cunning enough to create so many distractions like money, power, sports, fun etc. Such distractions have had the net impact of drawing our attention away from the things that really count—like focusing our attention on God through His creation. May He have mercy on us!

A Closer Look at Planet Earth

Planet Earth

It is the 3rd planet from the sun and the 5th largest in the Solar System. The earth is protected from the would-be damaging radiation from the sun. Its magnetic field protects it from

cosmic rays from the sun
while the ozone layer
that is 20-30 kilometers
above the earth
absorbs 97–99% of
ultraviolet light that
would be harmful to
God's creation. About
70 percent of the surface
of the earth is covered by
water just like 70 percent of a
human's body weight is made of water.

Hummingbird

The Earth rotates around the sun once every 365.26 days, a distance of about 150 million kilometers, and at the same time it rotates around its axis once every 24 hours.

The moon above, which is 384,000 kilometers from the earth, rotates around the earth every 27.32 days relative to the background stars. Since the earth also rotates around the sun, from new moon to new moon, it is about 29.53 days.

The sun, the moon and other heavenly wonders magnify God's awesome powers. The earth itself represents God's greatness. But the evil one has blinded us so that we don't see the majesty of the creation around us. If you doubt what I'm saying, take a moment to look at the grass, the trees, the shrubs, flowers and other plant types. Look at the birds as they fly, the butterflies, the creatures that crawl, the colorful fishes deep down in the seas. Then think of the lion, the elephant, the gazelle, the penguin and the panda. And finally look at the electrifying motion of the hummingbird, a small creature that can fly at over 50 kilometers per hour yet be able to hover mid-air and even fly backward. That little bird can even flap its wings at 20-30 flaps per second, 1500 per minute, which is pretty astonishing!

When you consider the wonders mentioned above, don't you come away with the feeling that God created man to worship and enjoy the beauty of the world? I certainly do. But beyond that, as we look forward to the second coming, we should fix our gaze on even greater wonders that will be ours to celebrate when we go to heaven.

In *Steps to Christ*, Page 2, Ellen G. White writes:

> *"God is love" is written upon every opening bud, upon every spire of springing grass. The lovely birds making the air vocal with their songs, the delicately tinted flowers in their perfection perfuming the air, the lofty trees of the forest with their rich foliage of living green—all testify to the tender fatherly care of our God and to His desire to make His children happy.*

I couldn't have said it better. Indeed God is love. The tragic thing is that many physicists and authorities in relevant disciplines have observed the greatness of the universe yet failed to appreciate the mind behind such wonders. Do such folk imagine that these things happened by chance? Do they really think the Big Bang theory is sufficient to explain the orderliness prevalent in the precision with which seasons come and seasons go in the universe? If you are like me, don't you sense that it would take a lot more faith to believe that things just happened rather than that a great God presided over the formation of the universe?

That brings me to a second issue. Why did the Lord bother to create so much if we were never going to understand His purposes? This is where it saddens my heart to see how the devil has skillfully distracted and manipulated our minds. It needs to be made clear that the Lord didn't engage in the business of creating such wonders to win accolades or mesmerize man and force worship. Far from it. The Lord did so for one reason only. LOVE. He loved man so much that He wanted us to be partakers in the joys and thrills of His creation.

And now for the sobering news—which we already flashed in chapter one. After He created all things and pronounced them good, He instituted a day of rest, which He called the Sabbath. Then He said, "Remember the Sabbath day and keep it holy!" The Lord didn't and does not ask much of man; He is simply asking that the love He's had for us be returned in worship to Him who created not only the heavens and the earth, but man as well.

As I conclude this chapter, I look at myself and ask God for forgiveness for my carelessness and recklessness as a steward of His creation. The question we must all ask ourselves is: Do we care enough about God's creation and about the environment in which we live? And do we see the flowers, the trees, the grass and all other creatures that are everywhere we go? If we don't, what does that say about our love for God?

We must remember that God loved man so much that He involved man in creation by asking man to give names to the wonders He had created. There could have been no greater calling than this. As it is written, God physically brought the wild animals and all the birds to be named by man.

Genesis Chapter 2:19 says this:

> *Now the Lord God had formed out of the ground all the wild animals and all the birds in the sky. He brought them to man to see what he would name them and whatever the man called each living creature, that was its name.*

Why did God do this? Why did He not go ahead and name all the good things He had created? The answer is LOVE.

We need to pray continually for the Lord to open our eyes so we can see and appreciate the wonders of creation!

CHAPTER 4

AND NOW GO TELL IT ON THE MOUNTAINS

This Call Isn't For The Fainthearted

The Lord does not want those of us who have been blessed to have come out of the blinding darkness this world has been plunged into to keep the light He has graciously shone on us to ourselves. He wants us to reach out to a dying world and proclaim it on the mountaintops that He alone is to be worshiped because He not only created the world, but redeemed it as well—when sin overran it. But being an omniscient God, He looked into the future and saw that man would not find this an easy task. Moses complained when he was called. David messed up in grand style when he was called. Abraham took matters into his hands to help God along. Knowing man would struggle to stay within the confines of the call, God talked to the prophet Jeremiah.

Listen to what God had to say in Jeremiah 1:4-5:

> *The word of the Lord came to me saying, 'Before I formed you in the womb I knew you, before you were born I set you apart. I appointed you a prophet to the nations.'*

Jeremiah was taken aback. If the text is to be interpreted, it appears as though God and Jeremiah had already had this conversation somewhere and now a persistent God was revisiting the subject. Jeremiah's response is indicative of His displeasure. He doesn't want to engage in this assignment. He says in Vs 6:

> *Alas, Sovereign Lord, I said I do not know how to speak; I am only a child.*

This is where I always find man amazing. Did Jeremiah know he was talking to the creator of the universe? Did he forget that the God who created the Milky Way and the Andromeda was the one talking to him? How could he complain about something as mundane as a tongue?

But the Lord was not about to get tough with him. Indeed, it is as if the Lord was pleading with him to see sense in what the Lord was asking him to do. If you please, we may at this point say that the Lord was asking Jeremiah to REMEMBER. He was saying:

> *Remember that I am the creator of all things, so with a touch or just a word from me your tongue will be turned into a tool of eloquence. So go!*

But of course the italicized words above are my imagination. Here is what the Lord actually said:

> *Do not say, 'I am only a child.' You must go to everyone I send you to and say whatever I command you.*

Remember that the Lord has a plan. To Him it does not matter at what age He sends one. Moses—the one whom the Lord knew face to face (Deuteronomy 34:10)—was asked to lead the children of Israel out of Egypt when he was 80 years old. Similarly, Joshua was called to take over from Moses and take the children of Israel into Canaan when he was advanced in age. What the Lord desires is that we each go to

Moses

the world and tell it on the mountains. He wants us to tell the world—REMEMBER!

But before we go, there is a matter that bothers both seasoned and newly called workers for the Lord. God's call is not a small matter. Indeed, those who weigh its magnitude right always shy away from the call. In this regard, Jeremiah—like Moses before him—is a case study. When he got the call, he took a measure of himself and fear washed through him. It's like he said, "Is God sure about this?"

"Yes," God said. "It's you I'm sending!"

"Me? But the people won't listen to me?"

This is where it gets interesting. Let's read God's response in Jeremiah 1:8:

> *Do not be afraid of them, for I am with you and I will rescue you.*

And regarding the children of Israel the Lord said, in Jeremiah 1:19: *They will fight against you but will not overcome you, for I am with you and will rescue you.*

Very reassuring. But the Lord wasn't done. Through Joshua, son of Nun, He comes down to our level and takes our hand. Before we read Joshua 1:5-7, let me make this point. I find it deeply reassuring that the Lord knows how challenging approaching people with the revolutionary massage of the cross and the Sabbath is. It is humbling that most people He called had the humility to see in the call mission impossible.

The reassuring thing was that the Lord reached out and said, "I will be with you always!"

And now let's look at God's words to Joshua.

> *No one will be able to stand up against you all the days of your life. As I was with Moses so I will be with you. I will not leave you nor forsake you wherever you go.*

Need I say more? No. First it is clear we must and GO TELL THE WORLD without fear that the Lord our God has commanded mankind TO OBSERVE THE SABBATH AND KEEP IT HOLY. Yes, this is a command!

God's Promise To The Faithful

The Lord is always watching and will ensure that what He has promised will come to pass. In Jeremiah 1:11-12, the prophet says:

> *The word of the Lord came to me. "What do you see, Jeremiah?" Jeremiah replied, "I see an almond tree"*
>
> *Then the Lord said to Jeremiah, "You have seen correctly, for I am watching to see that my word is fulfilled."*

The Lord Almighty is watching. His word does not change. So when he commands us to "Remember the Sabbath day and keep it holy," He means it. We must remember the Lord everyday of the week. But there is one day which He wants us to spend the whole day in remembrance of Him as our creator. That day is the Sabbath day, the day He sanctified.

May those who want to dilute and trivialize the Lord's significance and omnipotence be warned that celebration of the Lord's amazing grace began in the beginning and shall last forever. This story's end is already predicted.

So today, let us behold and have no fear for the Lord our God will be with all who proclaim His Word. Those who fear to tell the truth about God's law are like Jeremiah in his early years. They seem to be telling the Lord: "But I am only a child." And they say: "It is so difficult to tell anyone about the Sabbath" as they add: "One must be careful how we tell others about the Sabbath. You know it can be sensitive." They may even add: "I wish the pastor was with us to explain this Sabbath issue more clearly. That would help a lot."

We must learn to communicate better so we can weave into a credible narrative what we find challenging and difficult to tell others about. But even if we don't, the Lord has good news for us for He has promised: "Do not be afraid. I will be with you." Therefore, let us go and tell it on the mountains. All we have to do is to trust the Lord. Let us shout aloud and tell the truth without fear. Yes, the whole truth. The world must hear our voices as we shout: "REMEMBER!"

CHAPTER 5

CHRIST CONFIRMED THE SABBATH DAY

Christ said He came to fulfill all the commandments, not to void any. In His death and resurrection, He defined and confirmed the Sabbath rest as is highlighted in this chapter. Unlike the previous chapters, this one will take the shape of scriptural evidence of God's affirmation of the Sabbath. You may wonder why it is necessary to belabor the point that the Sabbath was instituted and sanctified by God, but that may only be because you haven't come face to face with people who dispute the authenticity of the signature on the Sabbath. To such folk, the only way to authenticate that signature is to have Christ sign it afresh—in their presence. That's the reason for this chapter.

Christ's Signature

Christ confirmed to all creation that the seventh day—after the Preparation Day, which is the 6th day—is the Sabbath of the Lord and that He arose on the first day of the week. Christ declared that He was the Lord of the Sabbath—the Sabbath that had been instituted at creation and further revealed to forgetful mankind, through the children of Israel. These were the people through whom the Lord had chosen to make Himself known to the lost world.

Now listen up—it is not a trivial matter that the Bible gives a chronology of events surrounding the death and resurrection of Christ. It is important to note that Christ, even though He is the Lord of the Sabbath, rested on that day in His tomb. This was a powerful example to man that the Sabbath was a day like no other. It was a day that humanity was called upon to reflect on the majesty and love of God—He who created the Milky Way and the Andromeda and the amazing creatures of the sea. Then in Mathew 12:8, Jesus declared, "For the Son of Man is the Lord of the Sabbath." And in Mark 2:27, He said, "Then he said to them, 'The Sabbath was made for man, not man for the Sabbath.'"

The two texts above may seem brief and even inconsequential in the broader scheme of things, yet a closer look at them reveal their foundational nature. The declaration is made that Christ is the Lord of the Sabbath, and that it was made for man. That being the case, how did it happen that man changed the day of worship? For the day of worship to have been changed, there needed to be three critical elements:

- A profound reason or shift in God's thinking. Such a shift would have been necessitated by a major crisis or something of that magnitude; because as I already pointed out, the seventh-day Sabbath is a foundational cornerstone in man's relationship with the Creator. For it to have been changed there had to have been a profound reason—and now we know there was none other than man's disobedience.

- God's authority (seal of approval). It is evident that there needed to be an express authority from God for the day of worship to be changed. The Bible could not have been silent on such a critical issue. Historians will tell you that for political and cultural issues, which had to do with the zero-sum power plays of the day, the

Roman authorities—working in concert with religious authorities of the time took it upon themselves to change the day of worship. This was egregious presumptuousness on their part. If it was God's desire to change His day of worship, He would have had this done in a sober, orderly manner, not under the pressure of debilitating persecution. Coercion is not God's style.

- Timeframe. This is where a clear reading of a book called *Genesis* is critical. In the book, the story of the beginning of time is told. In the opening chapters, what you see is a spellbinding narrative about how God created the heavens and the earth. But what you don't find spelt out clearly is the fact that by the end of that creation week something critical was established. It was *Time*. But the deal was—the time God seems to have added to the created world was an element that had already existed from eternity. It was God's way of proclaiming that the Sabbath—as a day of rest—would last from the beginning to eternity. Nobody would ever be allowed to change it. It is with this in mind that you have to wonder how arrogant and insensitive those who changed God's day of worship were. But what is even worse is that those who changed the day of worship know the profound impact of their deeds yet still preach such a foundational heresy. "Woe unto them!"

If you think those are tough words, it's because I intend them to have that very impact. It should be proclaimed far and wide that no human being can do anything about the Sabbath—no one can change or manipulate it. That's it!

Christ And The Sabbath

Now, let's get down to the book of Luke 4:16. In this narrative, what you need to come away with is how Christ handled the Sabbath. Here is the background. He went to Nazareth, where he had been brought up, and on the Sabbath day He went into the Synagogue, as was His custom. And he stood up to read the scripture from the book of Isaiah 61:1-2 (Luke 4:18-19). It reads:

> *The Spirit of the Lord is upon me, because he has anointed me to preach good news to the poor. He has sent me to proclaim freedom for the prisoners and recovery of sight for the blind, to release the oppressed, to proclaim the year of the Lord's favor.*

Then He went on to say in Luke 4:21 that:

> *Today this scripture is fulfilled in your hearing.*

It should not come as a surprise that Jesus chose a Sabbath day to preach this message. What better day was there to announce the fulfillment of prophecy than the Sabbath? Wasn't this what His signature was about? But He wasn't done writing it, let's carry on. As we do so, let us look at the crucifixion narratives by Mark, Mathew, Luke and John. It is important to point out that these men of God were direct witnesses, who were led by the Holy Spirit to give a detailed, firsthand account of what they saw, especially during Christ's crucifixion, burial and resurrection.

The Markan Account Of The Crucifixion

The death of Jesus on the cross, His burial and "rest" in the grave, and His resurrection on the third day, is the best definition of the Sabbath Day by the Bible. Let's take the Markan account in Mark 15.

> *Very early in the morning the chief priests, with the elders, the teachers of the law and the whole Sanhedrin, reached a decision. They bound Jesus, led him away and turned him over to Pilate.*

The verses that follow describe what took place up to the time of crucifixion.

The Sixth Day

It was the third hour when they crucified Him. In the sixth hour darkness came over the whole land until the ninth hour. And in that ninth hour Jesus cried in a loud voice, *"Eli, Eli, lama sabachthani?* – which means, "My God, my God, why have you forsaken me?" With a loud cry, Jesus breathed his last. So our Lord died.

Verses 42-43 say, "It was the Preparation Day (that is, the day before the Sabbath). So as evening approached, *vs. 43*, "Joseph of Arimathea, a prominent member of the Council, who was himself waiting for the kingdom of God, went boldly to Pilate and asked for Jesus' body." His intention was to bury the body before Sabbath set in. So Christ was buried as the evening approached on the sixth day—His first day in the tomb.

The Seventh Day (Sabbath)

The narrative rolls over into Mark 16:1. Here it says:

> *When the Sabbath was over, Mary Magdalene, Mary the mother of James and Salome bought spices so that they might go to anoint Jesus body.*

Do you see what's going on here? They had to wait till the Sabbath was over— that is after sunset—to buy the spices for there was no way they would have bought the spices on a Sabbath day. But the more significant point here is that Christ Himself rested on the Sabbath!

On The First Day (Sunday)

Let's read Mark 16:2:

> *Very early on the first day of the week, just after sunrise, they were on their way to the tomb and they asked each other, "Who will roll the stone away from the entrance of the tomb?"*

Let's skip the preliminaries and go down to verse 9. This verse is critical because it mentioned the days by order of their placement in the calendar of the time. It reads:

> *Jesus rose early on the first day of the week, He appeared first to Mary Magdalene, out of whom he had driven seven demons.*

Today all Christians celebrate Good Friday—the day Jesus died. They agree and recognize that He rose on the third day, the first day of the week—the day after the Sabbath. When you take this into account, you have to wonder what caused man to veer from the path of the true Sabbath to worshipping on a day the Lord had not instituted. By whose authority was this done? We will discuss this matter later.

The Mathew Account Of The Crucifixion

Mathew's account is found in chapter 27. Let's read it verse by verse:

> *vs.31*: Early in the morning, all the priests and the elders of the people came to the decision to put Jesus to death.
> *vs. 33*: They came to a place called Golgotha of the skull.
> *vs. 35*: When they had finished crucifying him, they divided up his clothes by casting lots.
> *vs. 45*: From the sixth hour until the ninth hour darkness came over the land.
> *vs. 46*: About the ninth hour Jesus cried out in a loud voice, *"Eli, Eli, lama sabachthani?"* – Which means, "My God, my God, why have you forsaken me?"
> *vs. 57*: As evening approached, there came a rich man from Arimathea, named Joseph, who had himself become a disciple of Jesus.
> *vs. 58*: Going to Pilate, he asked for the body of Jesus.
> *vs. 59*: Joseph took the body, wrapped it in a clean linen cloth, *vs. 60* and placed it in his own new tomb..."

Notice—without breaking the flow in this gripping narrative—that Mathew is careful to separate one day from another for the sake of clarity. This is important as we read on...

The seventh day (The Sabbath)

vs. 62*: The next day, the day after the Preparation Day,** the chief priests and the Pharisees went to Pilate, ***vs. 63 "Sir," they said, "we remember that while he was still alive that deceiver said, 'after three days I will rise again.'" ***Vs 64*:** So give the order for the tomb to be made secure until the third day. When I read such words I sometimes get so worked up. How dare they? Didn't they read their Bibles? Hadn't they witnessed the miracles? And even now—how could they fail to see in Christ the son of God? But that righteous anger is not the point of this discussion; let's get on to chapter 28.

Sunday (The first day of the week)

***vs. 1*:** "**After the Sabbath, at dawn on the first day of the week,** Mary Magdalene and the other Mary went to look at the tomb.
***vs. 2*:** There was a violent earthquake for an angel of the Lord came down from heaven and, going to the tomb, rolled back the stone and sat on it.
***vs 3*:** His appearance was like lightning and his clothes were white as snow. ***Vs 4*:** The guards were so afraid of him that they shook and became like dead men.
***vs. 5*:** The angel said to the women, "Do not be afraid, for I know that you are looking for Jesus, who was crucified.
***vs. 6*:** He is not here; he has risen, just as he said. Come and see the place where he lay. Jesus was risen from the dead!

The Lukan Account Of The Crucifixion

Day of Preparation (Friday)

The Book of Luke further reveals the Sabbath day. In Luke 23:50-52, it is written that a man named Joseph asked Pilate for the body of Jesus.

> ***vs. 52:*** Then he took it down, wrapped it in a linen cloth and placed it in a tomb cut in the rock, one in which no one had been laid.
> ***vs. 54:*** **It was the Preparation Day and the Sabbath was about to begin.** I've highlighted this verse because it makes an important point—that the Sabbath was about to begin at sunset on the Preparation Day.
> ***vs. 55:*** The woman who came with Jesus from Galilee followed Joseph and saw the tomb and how his body was laid in it.
> ***vs. 56:*** Then they went home and prepared spices and perfumes. **But they rested on the Sabbath in obedience to the commandment.**

The First Day (Sunday)

Luke 24:1 says:

> ***vs. 1:*** On the first day of the week, very early in the morning, the women took spices they had prepared and went to the tomb.
> ***vs. 6:*** He is not here, he has arisen! Remember how he told you, while he was still with you in Galilee, ***vs. 7*** that, "the Son of Man must be delivered into the hands

of sinful men, be crucified and on the third day be raised again?" What you see here is evidence that these people had never paid any attention to Christ's words. Does this happen to us today?

The Account Of John On The Crucifixion

Are you beginning to wonder just how long Christ's signature is? Indeed it is. It took four men to witness it. Having heard from three of the witnesses, it is only fair to hear what the fourth has to say. *John 19:31* says, "Now it was the Day of Preparation and the next day was to be a special Sabbath because the Jews did not want bodies left on the crosses during the Sabbath, they asked Pilate to have the legs broken. They broke the leg of the two people.

> *vs. 33*: But when they came to Jesus and found that he was already dead they did not break his legs.
> *vs. 34*: Instead one of the soldiers pierced Jesus' side with a spear bringing a sudden flow of blood and water. That Jesus was dead was not in doubt.
> *vs. 38*: Joseph of Arimathea asked Pilate for the body of Jesus.

―――

John 20:1: **Early on the first day of the week,** while it was still dark, Mary Magdalene went to the tomb...." The rest of the account is the same as what Mathew, Mark and Luke record. And so...what's their point?

The Point

The four writers were witnesses to Christ's signature as He wrote it to put His mark of authority on the Sabbath. In the modern world, for any case to be credible, witnesses are a crucial element of a fair trial. Though Christ is not under trial here, it was important to bring in those who watched Him handle the Sabbath to verify the fact that He did what He now asks us to do—to REMEMBER the Sabbath day and keep it holy. No, it wasn't fun for Him to stay buried under a grave named for someone, but I can assure you it was a joy to rest on the day His Father in heaven asked humanity to stop the activities of the past six days and reflect on higher things.

To those who have often claimed that Christ said little about the Sabbath in the New Testament, NOW YOU HAVE IT. Jesus didn't have to say anything because for Him, this was not an issue. Instead of speaking, He lived it. Therefore all mankind who are followers of Christ should follow Him.

Amen!

CHAPTER 6

THE DAY OF WORSHIP CHANGED

This is the chapter where we must now make a dramatic shift in tone and etiquette. There is no way to sanitize what we are going to discuss here without compromising the message or diluting it. It is written that Jesus worshipped on Sabbath Day and so did His apostles. For over 300 years after He was crucified, buried and resurrected, Christians worshipped on the Sabbath Day as was commanded by God. Peter, the apostle who some have claimed to have been "the first Pope," worshipped on the Sabbath Day. It has never been in our place to create a new reason for worship other than what is written in the Bible.

We have been commanded to remember, worship and honor the Lord as our Creator. This is the reason for God's declared Sabbath. The Lord looked back and saw that what He had made was good—the universe, the earth, the created beings on the face of the earth, in particular man, were all manifestations of His amazing love. God was pleased. What else could He say except to declare that man must remember Him as the Creator? What else could He do except to declare a day of rest for mankind? We may not have answers to these vexing questions, but one thing we know for sure is that the scriptures have not given a reason for a different day of worship nor suggested an alternative day to the Sabbath.

The origins of Sunday worship are clearly stated in the writings of the Catholic Church. Among these are the recordings of the various Synods that agreed on various *Laws* or *Canons.* In the

4th Century (the exact dates of the Synod remain unclear but it is believed that it took place in the year 363 or 364 AD), the Synod of Laodicea pronounced various canons, including Canon number 29, that stated as follows:

> "Christians must not judaize by resting on the Sabbath, but must work on that day, rather honoring the Lord's day; and, if they can, resting then as Christians. But if any shall be found to be judaizers, let them be anathema from Christ."

These changes in the day of worship, and hence in God's law, first came to light when Emperor Constantine issued an Edict in AD 321, instructing Christians and non-Christians to observe the **"venerable day of the sun"** which is Sunday, instead of the Sabbath Day. Constantine, who was the first Roman Emperor to convert to Christianity, ruled from 306 to 337 AD.

Let me take you back to the book of Genesis chapter 2 verses 1, 2 and 3:

> ***Vs. 1:*** Thus the heavens and the earth were completed in all their vast array.
> ***vs. 2:*** By the seventh day God had finished the work He had been doing; so on the seventh day he rested from all His work.
> ***vs. 3:*** And God blessed the seventh day and made it holy, because on it he rested from all the work of creating that He had done.

The Sabbath rest was thus instituted at creation. This, perhaps, is why God simply said, "Remember." It is therefore unthinkable for anyone to have declared that "Christians must not judaize by resting on the Sabbath." God declared Sabbath rest long before sin became a factor in man's life. This happened even before the children of Israel existed and thus the use of the word "judaize" is most inappropriate. The stubborn fact here is this—although the Catholic Church "changed" the day of worship, it had no choice but to acknowledge that the Sabbath Day (the seventh day, also known as Saturday) was God's original plan for man, but at its synodic meeting, it chose to change that day and instead gave the world Sunday as an alternative day for worship. The Synod of Laodicea, in Cannon number 16, declared:

> "The Gospels are to be read on the Sabbath [i.e. Saturday], with the other Scriptures."

This is further clarified in the Catholic Catechism. Para 2171, states:

> "God entrusted the Sabbath to Israel to keep as a sign of the irrevocable covenant. The Sabbath is for the Lord, holy and set apart for praise of God, his work of creation, and his saving actions on behalf of Israel."

But in a radical departure from this truth, the same Catechism, in Para 2174, goes on to say:

> "Jesus rose from the dead "on the first day of the week." Because it's the "first day," the day of Christ's resurrection recalled the first creation. Because it's the

"eight day" following the Sabbath, it symbolizes the new creation ushered in by Christ's Resurrection. For Christians, it has become the first of all days, the first of all feasts, the Lord's Day (he kuriake hemera, dies dominica)–Sunday. We all gather on the day of the sun, for it is the first day (after the Jewish Sabbath, but also the first day) when God, separating matter from darkness, made the world and on this same day, Jesus Christ our savior rose from the dead."

This doctrine from the Catholic Church gives a new reason for a day of worship that is contrary to what the Lord instructed. It is distressing to note that no attempt has ever been made to deny that the decision to change a creational (at creation of earth) day of worship was made by the authority of the church, as is evident in Canon 29, that was declared by the Synod of Laodicea. They didn't have such authority.

Further, when Constantine made the Edict of 321 A.D. he assumed authority in making this declaration. When he instructed Christians and non-Christians to observe the "venerable day of the sun," all the reasons given for the Sunday worship in the Catholic Catechism may not have been in Constantine's mind. In fact, by making reference to the "venerable day of the sun" one assumes that this was more to do with his desire to incorporate the sun-worshipers into Christian faith.

It is, however, important for all Christians to know that the Catholic Church acknowledges what they call the "Jewish Sabbath" as the Sabbath. The church simply decided to chose a different day of worship and is perhaps proud of it.

Let us turn once again to the Catholic Catechism.

In **Para 2175**, the Catechism states:

> "Sunday is extremely distinguished from the Sabbath which it follows chronologically every week; for Christians its ceremonial observance replaces that of the Sabbath…"

There you have it. The "change" in the day of worship has been clearly stated in the Catechism. But man did not just change the day of worship; he also changed the Ten Commandments to suit the change in his preferred day of worship. Let's look at the Catechism once more to make evident what we are saying here. What we seek to establish is that in the Catechism the second commandment has been omitted. This commandment states:

> *"You shall not make for yourself an image in the form of anything in heaven above or on the earth beneath or in the waters below.* **Vs 5** *You shall not bow down to them or worship them; for I, the Lord your God, I am a jealous God, punishing the children for the sin of the parents to the third and fourth generation of those who hate me,* **Vs 6** *but showing love to a thousand generation of those who love me and keep my commands."*

Because the Second Commandment has been omitted, the Fourth Commandment is named the third commandment and has been changed to read, "Remember to keep holy the Lord's Day."

Further, the Tenth Commandment has been split into two in the Catechism to keep the number ten as is highlighted in the table below which has been adapted using the NIV.

Table 1: The Ten Commandments and the Catechism (Ref: NIV and Catholic Church Catechism, Pages 496 – 497) **Note: The Catechism's English is British**

No.	Exodus 20: 2 – 17: The Bible Ten Commandments	Deuteronomy 5: 6 – 21: The Bible Ten Commandments	A traditional Catechical Formula: The Catholic Ten Commandments
1.	Vs 3: "You shall have no other gods before me	Vs 7: "You shall have no other gods before me.	I am the Lord your God; you shall not have strange gods before me. *(First Commandment)*
2.	Vs 4: "You shall not make for yourself an image in the form of anything in heaven above or on the earth beneath or in the waters below. Vs 5: You shall not bow down to them or worship them; for I, the Lord your God, I am a jealous God, punishing the children for the sin of the parents	Vs 8: "You shall not make for yourself an idol in the form of anything in heaven above or on the earth beneath or in the waters below. Vs 9 You shall not bow down to them or worship them; for I, the Lord your God, am a jealous God, punishing the children for the sin of the fathers	MISSING

	to the third and fourth generation of those who hate me, Vs 6 but showing love to a thousand generation of those who love me and keep my commands.	to the third and fourth generation of those who hate me, vs. 10 but showing love to a thousand generations of those who love me and keep my commandments.	
3.	Vs 7:"You shall not misuse the name of the Lord your God for the Lord will not hold anyone guiltless who misuses his name.	Vs 11: "You shall not misuse the name of the Lord your God, for the Lord will hold anyone guiltless who misuses his name.	You shall not take the name of the Lord your God in vain. *(Second commandment)*
4.	Vs: "Remember the Sabbath day by keeping it holy, vs. 9: six days you shall labour and do all your work, vs. 10 but the seventh day is a Sabbath to the Lord your God. On it you shall not do any work, neither you nor your son or daughter, nor your manservant, nor your animals,	Vs 12:"Observe the Sabbath day by keeping it holy, as the Lord your God has commanded you. Vs 13 Six days you shall labour and do all your work, vs. 14 but the seventh day is a Sabbath to the Lord your God. On it you shall not do any work, neither you, nor your son or	Remember to keep holy the Lord's Day. *(Third Commandment)*

	nor the alien within your gates. Vs 11 For in six days the Lord made the heavens and the earth, the sea, and all that is in them, but he rested on the seventh day. Therefore the Lord blessed the Sabbath and made it holy.	daughter, nor your manservant or maidservant, nor your ox, your donkey or any of your animals, nor the alien within your gates, so that your manservant and maidservant may rest, as you do. Vs 15 Remember that you were slaves in Egypt and that the Lord your God brought you out of there with a mighty hand and an outstretched arm. Therefore the Lord your God has commanded you to observe the Sabbath day.	
5.	Vs 12: "Honour your father and your mother so that you may live long in the land the Lord your God is giving you	Vs 16: "Honour your father and your mother as the Lord your God has commanded you, so that you may live long and that it may go well	Honor your father and your mother. *(fourth commandment)*

			with you in the land the Lord your God is giving you.	
6.	Vs 13: "You shall not murder	Vs 17: "You shall not murder		You shall not kill *(Fifth commandment)*
7.	Vs 14: "You shall not commit adultery	Vs 18: " You shall not commit adultery		You shall not commit adultery *(Sixth commandment)*
8.	Vs 15: "You shall not steal	Vs 19: " You shall not steal		You shall not steal *(Seventh commandment)*
9.	Vs 16: "You shall not give false testimony against your neighbour.	Vs 20: "You shall not give false testimony against your neighbour.		You shall not bear false witness against your neighbour *(Eighth commandment)*
10.	Vs 17: "You shall not covet your neighbour's house. You shall not covet your neighbour's wife, or his manservant or maidservant, or his ox or donkey, or anything that belongs to your neighbour."	Vs 21: "You shall not covet your neighbour's wife. You shall not set your desire on your neighbour's house or land, his manservant or maidservant, his ox or donkey, or anything that belongs to your neighbour."		You shall not covet your neighbour's wife. (Ninth commandment)
11				You shall not covet your neighbour's goods. *(Tenth commandment)*

The Eli Boys

In the book of 1ˢᵗ Samuel 3:12-14, the Lord has done something that makes it pertinent to discuss the implications of disobedience to God's desires here. The narrative is pretty chilling. Let me key in its main elements. These boys lived with their father in the temple, but were not cut of the same cloth as the old man. They loved life and refused to see God as their Creator. Because of this, the Lord rejected them and promised to punish them for generations to come. This is not something that should happen to anyone. I have sounded this warning here because continued disobedience to God's desire that we remember His Sabbath day of rest will invite His wrath upon us. This is an outcome we can all avoid by simply remembering and giving praise for the love He has bestowed upon us.

Before I conclude this chapter, let me say this—I have not alleged malice on the part of the ecclesiastical authorities who took it upon themselves to change God's commandments and day of worship; what I have done is wondered about their arrogance. Without any shred of authority from God they arrogated to themselves the power to alter God's plans and change the way man worshiped. To realize how serious this act was, consider that from the beginning of time God loved man. He wanted eternity to pass through our present age in a manner that upheld the foundational supremacy of the Sabbath as the day to worship Him. Let me sound a warning here: unless the people who presided over the sin of changing the day of worship repent and lead God's people back to the truth, they will realize too late that God's hand can't be twisted now just as it has never been twisted since the beginning of time.

The changing of the times and the Ten Commandments is predicted in the Bible. Daniel prophesied it would be done and gave us sufficient evidence to help us know when it would come to pass. The question therefore is—has it come to pass? Has the prophecy been fulfilled?

Let's read Daniel 7:24-25:

> **Vs.24:** The ten horns are the kings who will come from this kingdom. After them another king will arise; different from the earlier ones: he will subdue three kings.
> **Vs.25:** He will speak against the Most High and oppress His holy people and try to change the set times and the laws…"

And let us also read from Prophet Isaiah in the book of Isaiah 26:5:

> **Vs.5:** The earth is defiled by its people; they have disobeyed the laws, violated the statutes and broken the everlasting covenant.

Yes, we are disobedient. Man tried to change the laws and the set times, as we have seen in this chapter. The deluded man convinced himself that this could be done.

Isn't man pathetic? On the day the laws were "changed" I can imagine someone went home feeling good because he had changed the laws of the Almighty God. He felt like he was God. But here is a warning to anyone who thinks he/she can alter God's eternal laws and principles: **It Will Never**

Happen! If you doubt me, listen to Christ's own strident words in Mathew 5:

> **Vs.17** "Do not think that I have come to abolish the law or the prophets, I have not come to abolish them, but to fulfill them.
> **Vs.18** "For truly I tell you, until heaven and earth disappear, not the smallest letter, not the least stroke of a pen, will by any means disappear from the Law until everything is accomplished.
> **Vs.19** "Therefore anyone who breaks one of the least of these commandments and teaches others to do the same will be called least in the kingdom of heaven, but whoever practices and teaches these commands will be called great in the Kingdom of Heaven."

And then the final zinger:

> "If I had not come and spoken to them, they would not be guilty of sin. Now, however, they have no excuse for their sin" (John 15:22).

In other words, now that you know you should follow Christ and not act contrary to the revelation the Lord has so graciously given you. So do not follow man, follow the Lord Almighty. Sobering indeed!

CHAPTER 7

THE LAW AND GRACE

"Yes, salvation is by Grace and Grace alone!"

It was the beginning of time. The heavens and the earth did not exist. But God existed. The Father, the Son and Holy Spirit were there. One can only imagine what that moment was like when these words were pronounced: "Let us create the heavens and earth." It must have been a transfixing and monumental time. It had to have been a moment of divine soul-searching and a time to watch the unfolding of future events right from the beginning of time. When it was done, the Triune God declared all systems ready to go.

Creation started. In Genesis Chapter 1 verse 3, it is written:

> *Then God said, 'Let there be light;' and there was light.*

The Bible goes on to say in verse 4:

> *And God saw that the light was good; and he separated the light from darkness. God called the light Day and the darkness he called Night. And there was evening and there was darkness—the first day.*

And so A DAY was created. It had never existed before. When it started, time started too—from zero hours to eternity.

Before key pronouncements are made in this chapter, it should be clear that Time, comprising of Day and Night, was the first creation on day one. This fact is foundational in understanding that God is a God of order. He planned everything from zero hour and anticipated how systems in the universe would relate one with another as the pivots of time revolved around Love.

When time was created, it was made universally available and accessible to all creation. Each creation, during a life time, has time in equal measure. The 24-hour day cycle was designed by God to be the same for all His creation. It is the jewel that was freely given without preference.

The Lord Almighty declared this in Jeremiah 33 verse 20:

> **Vs 20:** *If you can break my covenant with the day and my covenant with the night, so that day and night no longer come at their appointed time,*
>
> **Vs 21:** *then my covenant with David my servant—and my covenant with the Levites who are priests ministering before me—can be broken and David will no longer have a descendant to reign on his throne.*

But we know that God's word and God's covenant cannot be broken. And it is unthinkable that a created human being can even contemplate changing, altering or misinterpreting the word of God.

In this chapter, we discuss the Law and Grace. There are many today who have been misled to believe that the "Law of Moses" has been abolished because "Grace has come." Anyone who accepts this teaching has been deceived. God's law cannot be changed through interpretation or misinterpretation of God's word by man. Jesus said He came to fulfill the law. He had no sin. He kept all commandments including the Fourth, on the Sabbath, even unto death.

In His own words, Jesus said this in Mathew 5 verses 17-19:

> ***Vs 17:*** *Do not think that I have come to abolish the Law of the Prophets; I have come not to abolish them but to fulfill them.*
>
> ***Vs 18:*** *I tell you the truth, until heaven and earth disappear, not the smallest letter, nor the least stroke of a pen, will by any means disappear from the law until everything is accomplished.*
>
> ***Vs 19:*** *Anyone who breaks one of the least of these commandments and teaches others to do the same will be called least in the kingdom of heaven, but whoever practices and teaches these commands will be called great in the kingdom of heaven.*

That's Jesus speaking. He did not say at any time that because of His coming, the law was no longer valid. He fulfilled the law. He told everyone to hold on to His teachings. But again, this is another critical matter on which I'd rather let Christ speak to you in His own words. Here He is in John chapter 8 verses 31 and 32:

> ***Vs 31:*** To the Jews who had believed in Him, Jesus said, 'If you hold to my teaching, you are really my disciples.
>
> ***Vs 32:*** Then you will know the truth, and the truth will set you free.'

Our savior has opened our eyes through His life of teaching, death and resurrection. Through His death we have been saved by grace and grace alone.

The Lord goes on to make this conditional pronouncement in John 14 verse 15:

If you love me, you will obey what I command.

But again, it is not by our own effort that we keep the commands; we can only do so through Him who died for us. In John 14 verse 16 Christ explains how this was to be done. Let's read:

> **Vs 16:** *And I will ask the Father, and He will give you another Counselor to be with you forever*
>
> **Vs 17:** *the Spirit of the truth. The world cannot accept Him, because it neither sees Him nor knows Him. But you will know Him, for He lives with you and will be in you.*
>
> **Vs 18:** *I will not leave you as orphans; I will come to you.*

This is the fulfillment of God's promise to the children of Israel and by extension to all humanity as is written in Ezekiel 11 verse 19 – 20. The words here are so important that I want us to read them together:

> **Vs 19:** I will give them an undivided heart and put a new spirit in them; I will remove from them their heart of stone and give them a heart of flesh.
>
> **Vs 20:** Then they will follow my decrees and be careful to keep my laws. They will be my people, and I will be their God. And this is the

truth: The Spirit in us will cause us to follow God's commandments.

The Apostle Paul's Message

Let me now turn to one of the most misinterpreted texts in the Bible. In the book of Galatians, the Apostle Paul said this in chapter 3 verses 23 and 24:

Vs 23: *Before faith came, we were held prisoners by the law, locked up until faith should be revealed.*

Vs 24: *So the law was put in charge to lead us to Christ that we might be justified by faith.*

Vs 25: *Now that faith has come, we are no longer under the supervision of the law.*

Paul was speaking to the Galatians, who seemed to have turned away from the gospel of Christ. But it is the words he uses in Galatians 4:6 that any reader will find confounding. His injudiciousness is calculated to make a strong point—and it does. Let's read:

I am astonished that you are so quickly deserting the one who called you by the grace of Christ and are turning to a different gospel—which is really no gospel at all. Evidently some people are throwing you into confusion and are trying to pervert the gospel of Christ.

Paul was clearly agitated at this point. So furious was he that in Galatians 3:1-2 he dropped diplomacy and screamed, *"You foolish Galatians! Who has bewitched you? Before your very eyes Jesus Christ was clearly portrayed as crucified. I would like to learn just one thing: Did you receive the Spirit by observing the law or by believing what you heard? Are you so foolish? After beginning by the Spirit, are you now trying to attain your goal by human effort?"*

Yes, Paul was seething, but if you read Galatians 2 verse 15-16 in context, you'll quickly realize that what he was saying had to be said—and he is pretty sober at this point. Listen to his return to diplomacy:

> *We who are Jews by birth and not Gentile sinners know that man is not justified by observing the law, but by faith in Jesus Christ. So we, too, have put our faith in Christ Jesus that we may be justified by faith in Christ and not by observing the law, because by observing the law no one can be justified.*

This was Paul's strongest assertion that salvation came through grace and not by works. He was evidently not saying that the law "has been done away with" and in its place "grace has taken over." No at all. His position is made even clearer when his words to the Galatians are played alongside his words to the Romans. In Romans 6 verses 1-2 he asks a question that adds to the weight of his words to the Galatians. He says:

> *What shall we say then? Shall we go on sinning so that grace may increase? By no means! We died to sin; how can we live in it any longer?*

What Then Is Sin?

It is necessary to point out that sin is defined by God's Commandments. To underscore this fact, let us look at what Paul says in Roman 7 verse 7:

What shall we say, then? Is the law sin? Certainly not! Indeed I would not have known what sin was except through the law. For I would not have known what coveting really was if the law had not said "Do not covet". And this is still the case for us today.

Further, it must be emphasized that without sin there would be no need for grace. In fact, grace immediately came into effect after the fall of man when God put in place the plan for salvation. After Adam and Eve sinned, the Lord told the serpent in Genesis 3:15 that, "And I will put enmity between you and the woman, and between your offspring and hers, he will crush your head and you will strike his heel." This is in direct reference to Christ's triumph over Satan and Christ's death on the cross to bring salvation to fallen, undeserving man. This is unmerited favor. Grace!

The Law Of Moses

God's Law, the Ten Commandments, were passed down to mankind through His servant, Moses. These laws will remain in effect until Jesus comes to take us home. After this, there will be no need for anyone to be told not to sin because those who join Christ in heaven and in the new earth will not sin again as the enemy will have been defeated. The work of grace will have been accomplished. However, one commandment will remain—worshipping the Lord Our God on the Sabbath as it is written in the book of Isaiah chapter 26 verses 22-23:

> **Vs 22:** *As the new heavens and the new earth that I will make will endure before me, declares the Lord, so will your name and descendants endure.*

Vs 23: *From one New Moon to another and from one Sabbath to another, all mankind will come and bow down before me," says the Lord.*

Until then, the Law remains in effect. Let no one deceive you that because we have Grace you are free to go on coveting other people's wives, stealing other people's property and lying as you please, just to mention three of the Ten Commandments. There is no such freedom. Of course, we know that on our own it is impossible to obey and that is why we need the Holy Spirit to dwell in us, in Jesus name, and cause us to obey. It is evident that even if we tried to obey we would still remain sinners, hence the need for salvation by grace. We must also remember that throughout the Bible, God does not like disobedience. In the new heaven and new earth there will be no place for disobedience. There will be no sin and there will be no need for the Law.

Mount Sinai

It was on Mount Sinai where the Lord met Moses as he journeyed with the House of Jacob across the Desert of Sinai. It was in the third month after the Israelites left Egypt. The Israelites had camped in front of the mountain as Moses went up to talk to the Lord. There, the Lord told Moses to tell the Israelites what is recorded in Exodus 19:4-5. Let's read:

Vs 4: *You yourselves have seen what I did to Egypt, and how I carried you on eagles' wings and brought you to myself.*

Vs 5: *Now if you obey me fully and keep my covenant, then out of all nations you will be my treasured*

> *possession. Although the whole earth is mine, you will be for me a kingdom of priests and a holy nation.*

Moses passed on to the Israelites the message from God. The Israelites responded positively saying, "We will do everything the Lord has said." So Moses went back to the Lord and reported what he had been told. It is evident that the Lord was pleased for He told Moses to go back to the Israelites and tell them to consecrate themselves by washing their clothes and get ready to meet Him (God) in three days.

Exodus 19:14-15 says:

> *After Moses had gone down the mountain to the people, he consecrated them, and they washed their clothes. Then he said to the people, "Prepare yourselves for the third day. Abstain from sexual relations.*

Mount Sinai was covered with smoke as the Lord descended to meet the people of Israel. There was thunder and lightning and the people trembled as they gathered at the foot of the mountain. The mountain shook violently and there was the sound of trumpet that grew louder and louder. This was an awesome setting. The Lord was about to speak to His Children and to give His commandments. The Lord finally handed over the Ten Commandments to Moses as outlined in Exodus 20.

As Moses was getting the Law directly from God on Mount Sinai, the Israelites grew impatient. In Exodus 32 verse 1 it is written: "When the people saw that Moses was so long in coming down from the mountain, they gathered around Aaron and said, 'Come, make us gods who will go before us. As for this fellow Moses who brought us up out of Egypt, we don't know what has happened to him.'"

This is difficult to comprehend. In spite of what they had seen performed by the Lord through His servant, Moses, they referred to Moses as "this fellow." They were full of contempt and certainly showed no love for the Lord.

But it's even more difficult to understand why Aaron, Moses' brother and an anointed priest, succumb to these demands. Aaron did not delay in asking the Israelites to remove their gold earrings; he personally took these earrings, as it is written in exodus 32:4, and fashioned out a calf. Let's read the account in verse 4:

> *He took what they handed him and made it into an idol cast in the shape of a calf, fashioning it with a tool. Then they said, 'These are your gods, O Israel, who brought you up out of Egypt.'*

Can you believe this? Aaron even went ahead and built an altar for the idol!

The Lord was disobeyed by His chosen people of Israel. They broke one of the Ten Commandments—making an idol, bowing and worshiping it—even before they received the tablet Moses had brought down from the Mountain. And so Exodus 32:7-8 says:

> **Vs 7:** *Then the Lord said to Moses, 'Go down, because your people, whom you brought up out of Egypt, have become corrupt.*

> ***Vs 8:*** *They have been quick to turn away from what I commanded then and have made themselves an idol cast in the shape of a calf. They have bowed down to it and sacrificed to it and have said, 'these are your gods, O Israel, who brought you out of Egypt.'*

Even today, human beings are quick to make idols and images for themselves in direct disobedience to God. This situation is reinforced by those who proclaim that the law has been done away with. Many shy away from telling people what the law says. No wonder people are not aware of the new idols they worship and bow to. There are images and idols, even in churches, which people revere. Today people have turned to worshiping and idolizing sports teams and sports men and women, for example. People worship their properties and they worship money.

But how can anyone say that the law has been abolished? Take a look at the first two commandments, which were broken by the Israelites at the foot of Mount Sinai. We get the record in Deuteronomy chapter 20 verses 3 and 4:

> ***Vs 3:*** *You shall have no other gods before me (First Commandment).*

> ***Vs 4:*** *You shall not make for yourself an idol in the form of anything in heaven above or on the earth beneath or in the waters below.*

> ***Vs 5:*** *You shall not bow down to them; for I, the Lord your God, am a jealous God, punishing the children for the sin of the fathers to the third and fourth generation of those who hate me;*

Vs 6 *but showing love to a thousand generations, of those who love me and keep my commandments (Second Commandment).*

These laws remain valid until the end of time, when Christ comes to take His children home. For we are under command not to have other gods and anyone who stands in a pulpit to declare that these laws have been abolished has been deceived. The laws are to be kept. What is different is the way we are able to keep them. In the days of Moses, the Lord led Israelites by the hand and gave them the command to obey. They had to make an effort to do so and would be punished instantly if they did not. But today we have the Holy Spirit in us to help us follow God's word and to keep His commandments. All we have to do is believe and ask in the name of Jesus and it will be done unto us as we have asked.

The children of God can be overcomers. As it is written in Revelation 12 verse 11:

> *They overcame by the blood of the Lamb and by the word of their testimony..."*

And in verse 17:

> *Then the dragon was enraged at the woman and went off to make war against the rest of her offspring – those who obey God's commandments and hold to the testimony of Jesus.*

It is evident that verse 17 is answered by verse 11. Those who held the faith *overcame*. Obedience to God comes from the Lord Himself. Those who are in Christ will be obedient to the Lord. When we love the Lord, He will bless us. What we must not do is to try and earn our way into heaven. This we leave to the Lord our God. He is all-knowing and His Grace is sufficient.

Jesus Magnifies The Law

Jesus addressed the various laws that were part of the Ten Commandments. Contrary to the assertions of those who say that the law was abolished when grace came, Jesus went ahead and told His disciples about the law. In fact, He magnified the law. For example, He said in Mathew chapter 5:

> ***Vs 21:*** *You have heard that it was said to people long ago, 'Do not murder, and anyone who murders will be subject to judgment.*
>
> ***Vs 22:*** *But I tell you that anyone who is angry with his brother will be subject to judgment.'*
>
> ***Vs 27:*** *You have heard that it was said, 'Do not commit adultery.*
>
> ***Vs 28:*** *But I tell you that anyone who looks at a woman lustfully has already committed adultery with her in his heart.'*

When a Pharisaic expert of the law tested Jesus with the question, "Teacher, which is the greatest commandment in the law?" Jesus said these words in Mathew 22 verses 37-40:

> ***Vs 37:*** *Love the Lord your God with all your heart and with all your soul and with all your mind. This is the first and greatest commandment.* ***Vs 38****: And the second is like it: 'Love your neighbor as yourself.'* ***Vs 40****: All the Law and the Prophets hang on these two commandments.*

The Law in its entirety hangs on these two statements. And in these statements Jesus confirm that the Ten Commandments matter. The first four of the Ten Commandments are summarized in **"Love the Lord your God with all your heart and with all your soul and with all your mind."** For if one loves the Lord in the manner Jesus is saying then one will:

- Have no other gods (First Commandment).
- Make no idols and do not bow down to any idol (Second Commandment).
- Not misuse the name of the Lord our God (Third Commandment), and
- Remember to keep the Sabbath day by keeping it holy (Fourth Commandment).

Similarly, when Jesus says, **"Love your neighbor as yourself,"** He is evidently reminding us that one must:

- Honor his or her father and mother (Fifth Commandment)
- Not commit murder (Sixth Commandment)
- Not commit adultery (Seventh Commandment)
- Not steal (Eight Commandment)
- Not give false testimony (Ninth Commandment), and
- Not covet their neighbor's house or wife, or anything that belongs to their neighbor (Tenth Commandment).

I don't understand how anyone in his or her right mind can say that any of the above commands have been abolished. Take a second look at the Ten Commandments paraphrased above. Read them again and see how intrinsically interwoven they are with the tenets of natural coexistence of the human race, nature and the environment. Let us hold on to the truth and the truth will set us free!

The New Covenant

As has been stated already in this book, many people have been deceived that in the "new covenant" the Law has been abolished and in its place grace has been instituted. Whereas it is true that we are under grace and cannot earn our way to heaven by simply observing the law, it is also true that God's command that we keep His laws has not been changed.

Having said this, it is clear that many things changed with the coming of Christ. I have made an attempt to summarize some of these changes in the table below:

Table: The old and the New

During the time of Moses	After Jesus' first coming
When the Lord led the Children of Israel out of Egypt to Canaan, He "held them by the hand" and watched over them, commanding them to keep God's commandments which He gave through Moses.	Jesus came and before returning to the Father after crucifixion said that He would ask the Father to send the Holy Spirit to live in our hearts. The Spirit would cause us to observe God's commandments.
Deuteronomy 6 vs 25: "If we are careful to obey all this law before the Lord our God, as He has commanded us, that	Ephesians 2 vs 8: "For it is by grace you have been saved through faith–and this not from yourselves, it is the gift of God–

will be our righteousness."	vs 9: not by works, so that no one can boast".
Righteousness by works	Righteousness by faith
Deuteronomy 27 vs 26: "Cursed is the man who does not uphold the words of this law by carrying them out".	Galatians 3 vs 13: Christ redeemed us from the curse of the law by becoming a curse for us, for it is written: Cursed is everyone who is hung on a tree."
People could be stoned to death for violation of the law.	Sinners who will not have been saved through God's grace will await final judgment at the end of time.
Sacrifices were to be offered as people sought forgiveness of sins.	No more need for sacrifices. Christ died for all on the cross and atoned for our sins.
There was belief in circumcision and other traditions which were also demanded of the gentiles as well.	It is the heart that needs "circumcision". Faith in Christ is enough. Galatians 6 vs 15: "Neither circumcision nor uncircumcision means anything, what counts is new creation"
In Deuteronomy 19 verses 19 – 21 Moses said: "...You must purge the evil from among you. The rest of the people will hear about this and will be afraid and never again will such an evil be done among	Jesus said in Mathew 5 verses 38 –41: "You have heard that it was said, 'Eye for eye and tooth for tooth'. But I tell you, do not resist an evil person. If someone strikes you on the right cheek, turn to him the other also. And

you. Show no pity: life for life, eye for eye, tooth for tooth, hand for hand, foot for foot"	if someone wants to sue you and take your tunic, let him have your cloak as well. If someone forces you to go a mile, go with him two miles.
The additional rules and regulations were passed on to Moses. As the Israelites settled in Canaan, these additional rules would help them leave more peacefully and avoid contacting diseases many of which were incurable at the time.	Most of these rules and regulations were no longer necessary.

In concluding this chapter, it is important to remind ourselves that grace came so that the law would not be a burden to us. One can no longer stone anyone for committing adultery as was the case in the days of Moses. And we are not saved because we have no sin. Indeed "… all have sinned and fall short of the glory of God" (Romans 3:23). Sin will only be done away with in the end when Christ returns to take us home.

Our Lord Jesus Christ has died for our sins and has made it possible for us to be saved, not because we are righteous, but because the Lord loves us. However, we are asked to have understanding and hate sin. But we can only hate sin if we know what sin is, hence the Ten Commandments. To drive this point home, the Apostle Paul, in Romans 3:20, says: *Therefore no one will be declared righteous in his sight by observing the law; rather, through the law we become conscious of sin.*

We are called to be obedient unto the Lord our God and to keep His commandments. This obedience will come to those who love the Lord and who open their hearts to Christ, who is willing and is standing at the door.

CHAPTER 8

YOU ARE THE APPLE OF GOD'S EYE

Whoever touches you touches the
Apple of God's eye

The Lord our God made man out of His unselfish love—in His own image. God was pleased with what He had made and declared it "very good." There is no one in heaven or on earth who can make a fly or an ant for these are complex beings. So when the Lord looked at the universe and all that was in it He was pleased and desired that all mankind should honor Him and not forget the marvelous act of creation. He commanded man NOT TO FORGET, but to REMEMBER Him as the Creator.

Of all His creation, God loved man the most. The rest of creation in the universe was spoken into being, but man was made by hand. And therefore when man sinned and suffered separation from God, the Lord set in motion a plan to save man. John 3:16 puts it best:

For God so loved the world that he gave his one and only Son, that whoever believes in him shall not perish but have eternal life (NIV).

That remains one of the most powerful and popular verses in the Bible—for obvious reasons. It talks about that one force that has proved elusive in man's life—LOVE. The point it makes is this: mankind must know that the Lord loves us dearly and calls on us to take refuge in Him even as we await His second coming. As it is written, let us "taste and see that the Lord is good; blessed is the man who takes refuge in him (Psalms 34:8).

Having delved into a number of issues in the early chapters, it is in order for us to consider quotes and texts in the Bible that build our faith in God's plan for our salvation. Our faith is built by knowing He will protect us because of His loving grace. In this respect, let's get started with the words of Isaiah, one of the prophets who zeroed-in-on the importance of God's love. He called upon all those who are thirsty to come to the waters. Let's read:

> *Come all you who are thirsty, come to the waters; come buy and eat. Come buy wine and milk without money and without cost* (Isaiah 55:1).

The Lord calls because He knows we are His pearl. But what does that mean? Does it mean He will shield us from harm always? Will He always protect us from harm and danger and death? To understand what God is saying, we have to consider the words placed in the Bible designed to reassure us that He watches over us even when we fail to keep His precepts. In what Deuteronomy calls **the apple of His eye**, let's find the first reassurance.

It says in Chapter 32:10-12 that:

> *In a desert's land he found him, in a barren and howling waste, He shielded him and covered him; he guarded him as the apple of his eye....*

Following in Moses' footsteps, David says:

Keep us as the apple of your eye; hide me in the shadow of your wings (Psalms 17:8).

But it is probably Zacharia, who had to contend with the difficult issues of war and death, who had to reassure the Israelites of God's abiding protection. In one of the most pointed phrases, he says in Zacharia 2:8 that:

> *For this is what the Lord Almighty says, "After he has honored us and he has sent me against the nations that have plundered you – for whoever touches you touches the apple of His eye."*

The apple of God's eye is a powerful analogy indeed, but it must not be what we focus on. Our focus should remain on the fact that the Lord—He who created the Milky Way and the Andromeda—would come down to our level and protect us from the evil designs of others. I don't think it is a small matter that God would call us the apple of His eye. Is it any wonder He sent His only son to die on the cross for us? And is it any wonder that His keen interest in us makes Him know even the count of hair on our heads? (Mathew 10:30). *So don't be afraid; you are worth more than many sparrows (vs31).*

Having given such a strong reassurance, Christ Himself concludes His earthly ministry by saying words of eternal value. In John 14:27 He says:

> *Peace I leave with you; my peace I give you. I do not give to you as the world gives. Do not let your hearts be troubled and do not be afraid.*

But should the burdens of the world prove too heavy, should persecution come our way for proclaiming the good news of Sabbath rest, Christ says, in Mathew 11:29-31 that:

> **vs29** *Come to me all you who are weary and burdened and I will give you rest.* **vs30** *Take my yoke upon you and learn from me. For I am gentle and humble in heart, and you will find rest for your souls.* **vs31** *For my yoke is easy and my burden is light.*

In the light of a text like the one above, many have looked at the world today and wondered what Christ meant. Has His burden really been light? If you look at the flowers, the birds, the antelope, the fish in the deep of the sea, the trees, the grass, the stars, the heavens, the earth, the ants, the bees, the frogs and other creations, what you see is glory. Indeed it is. But when you look at the ravages of war and tsunamis and earthquakes and desertification and other environmental catastrophes, you have to wonder about Christ's words. Was He aware such calamities would take place? How did He imagine they would affect our understanding of His love for us? To answer that question, let's consider the creation of man.

The Creation Of Man

There are two things God did that undoubtedly prove His love for man. One was creation. The other was redemption. Though both are tied intimately to the Sabbath, I want us to once again consider creation and its bearing on God's love for man. To do this, we have to look at the book of Genesis 1:27-28. Let's read together:

> *So God created man in his own image, in the image of God created he him; male and female created he them. And God blessed them and said to them Be fruitful and increase in number; fill the earth and subdue it. Rule over the fish of the sea and the birds of the air and over every living creature that moves on the ground.*

God's love is not manifested in the fact that He created, but in how He did it. He used His hands to mold man into the perfect creature He wanted man to be. But it didn't end there. He took care to ensure that man was created in God's own image. Do you see the significance of this? This was God telling man that He loved man. Because of such love, He was willing to place everything He created under the care of man. And so He said:

> *Behold, I have given you every herb bearing seed, which is upon the face of all the earth, and every tree…* (vs29)

Do you realize what's going on here? This wasn't just love. It was trust as well. God recreated heaven here below and made man in charge. If this wasn't love, what is? This is the same God who now asks us to REMEMBER His creative power and love for us. He wants us to proclaim His goodness everywhere we may be. As we remember His wonderful act of creation, as we commemorate His selflessness daily, we must also remember that taking care of ourselves is a glorious act that gives glory to Him. It is an acknowledgement of the wonderful gift of life He has bestowed upon us.

Recognizing God's love that made Him touch man with His hands, we should not abuse our bodies. We should never put into the body anything that intoxicates it. It's not part of God's plan to have the body intoxicated. Our bodies are not dustbins. We have to avoid harmful things, because in the long run it amounts to the same situation Eve found herself in when the serpent asked, "Did God really say you must not eat from any tree in the garden?" (Genesis 3:1)

Eve defended herself in Genesis 3:3:

> *But God did say 'you must not eat fruit from the tree that is in the middle of the garden, and you must not touch it, or you will die'*

Satan responded in 3:4:

> *You will not certainly die.*

Do you see what's going on here? Our rebellion even on matters of temperance started right there in the Garden of Eden. It's like Satan is still telling people today, *Eat for everything made by God is good and will not harm you.* And foolishly, like Adam and Eve, we eat and drink and intoxicate our bodies. We fail to remember that the body is the temple of God (1 Cor. 3:16), and that we are the apple of God's eye.

- We smoke
- We intoxicate our bodies with alcohol
- We take drugs
- We eat forbidden foods such as pork
- We abuse sex

These acts grieve the Holy Spirit, who must wait for us while we indulge. Indeed, it's like telling the Holy Spirit, "Wait for me while I do this act, then we can talk later." The good news is that God is love and He is always forgiving. But be careful when you keep sending the Holy Spirit away to wait in the parking lot for there will come a day when there is no more parking space in the parking lot. By the way, wasn't this what happened during the days of Noah? Let's get the story in Genesis 5:32. Noah was 500 years old when he became father to Shem, Ham and Japheth. You may read the rest of the account. For now, let me jump to Genesis 6:1, that says:

> *When human beings began to increase in number on earth and daughters were born to them, the sons of God saw that the daughters of human beings were beautiful and they married any of them they chose.*

Then the Lord said,

> *"My Spirit will not contend with humans forever, for they are mortal; their days will be a hundred and twenty years."*

The Spirit of God could no longer go to the parking lot to wait for God's children as they engaged in immoral and sinful acts and the years of their children were shortened. I have added this anecdote to this narrative only to make the point that in the Sabbath rest, the Lord created a covenant with man that was all-encompassing. By entering into the Sabbath rest—which was to be at peace with God on a daily basis—man was created with the ability to remain sinless even this side of eternity. The formula is the Sabbath!

CHAPTER 9

YOU ARE FORGIVEN

We have covered a lot of ground in the chapters ahead of this one. Because of the gap that has existed between man and God, there may be a tendency by man to despair, to feel as though it is hopeless to try a comeback to where the Lord wants us to be. In this chapter, I introduce to you a God who stands ready to forgive your past and start you on a new path. He is the God who made the heavens and the earth and everything therein. He is the God who led the children of Israel out of Egypt and split the Red Sea for them to walk on dry land, between the walls of the waters of River Jordan, as the fish cheered and flapped their fins.

The Lord is the God who spoke to Moses and handed him the Ten Commandments on Mount Sinai. He is the one who told Joshua (Joshua Chapter 1:5) this:

> *No one will be able to stand up against you, all the days of your life. As I was with Moses, so I will be with you, I will never leave you nor forsake you.*

So when Joshua later prayed for the sun to stand still while the children of Israel engaged in battle against the Amorites, God answered Joshua. For it is written in Joshua chapter 10:13 that:

> *So the sun stood still, and the moon stopped, till the nation avenged itself on its enemies, as it is written in the Book of Joshua. The sun stopped in the middle of the sky and delayed going down a full day.*

This is the God who before He gave Moses the two Tables of the Testimony, said to Moses, in Exodus 31:13 that the Sabbath was a crucial covenant.

Let's read:

Say to the Israelites, 'You must observe my Sabbaths. This will be a sign between me and you for the generations to come, so you may know that I am the Lord, who makes you holy.'

Notice how the Lord talks about **my Sabbaths**. Back in time, when the children of Israel complained about food as the Lord led them through the desert land, the Lord told Moses, in Exodus 16, what was to be done to honor Him. Let's consider all the crucial verses in this regard:

Vs4 *I will rain down bread from heaven for you. The people are to go out each day and gather enough for that day. In this way, I will test them and see whether they will follow my instructions.*
Vs5 *On the sixth day they are to prepare what they bring in and that is to be twice as much as they gathered on other days. So each one gathered as much as they needed for each day.*
Vs22 *On the sixth day they gathered twice as much, two omers for each person, and the leaders of the community came and reported this to Moses.*
Vs23 *This is what the Lord commanded: 'Tomorrow is the day of Sabbath rest, a holy Sabbath to the Lord. So bake what you want and to bake and what you want to boil.*
Vs26 *Six days you are to gather it, but on the seventh day, the Sabbath, there will not be any.*

It is very clear that the Lord revealed to the children of Israel which day was the Sabbath and why it was to be observed. And as we have already seen, Jesus—in His death, burial and resurrection—confirmed this to His followers in the New Testament and through the ages.

So do we have any excuse not to remember?

The answer is no. The same God who spoke to Moses and Joshua is the same God who has spoken to us through His word. He is the Lord Almighty who is the same yesterday, today and tomorrow. He is the ONE who changeth not. And He is the ONE who has commanded us to keep all His commandments, including the 4th Commandment. In doing this, He pleads with us to REMEMBER.

The Lord is saying this to mankind:

> *I am the Lord your God. I created you from dust. You are mine and I love you. I am the one who spoke to Moses and to the children of Israel. So today listen to me. You shall worship me and me alone. You must remember me as your creator. And because I love you, I will help you to obey all my commandments.*

These are the words of God!

Ten Commandments

Aren't those sweet words? Aren't they reassuring? Truth is that we now know there is nowhere in the Bible where the day of worship was changed. Further, all Christians and non-Christians must know there is nowhere in the Bible where Sunday is referred to as the day of worship. We know that Christ arose on Sunday, fine, but this does not give us any permission to change the basis for the weekly Sabbath worship. In fact, this should strengthen our faith as we know that Christ rested in His grave on the Sabbath and arose "on the first day of the week."

To Christians who worship on Sundays, I want to say this as gently as I can. **You have been deceived.** And to Christians who worship on God's Sabbath but do not keep it holy, **you have been deceived even more.** The tragedy here is knowing the truth, but not abiding by it. It were better if we hadn't known the truth in the first place—that way the Lord would have mercy on us!

But there is GOOD NEWS for all of us. Christ died on the cross so we could be forgiven. It is written in Romans Chapter 3:23 that: *For all have sinned and fallen short of the glory of God.*

The point of that verse is this—we are all sinners. We should not judge ourselves or judge others; we should let God be the judge. Indeed, we now know we shall be held accountable by God. But remember the good news: ***Christ died for you and me so that we can be forgiven.*** It is written in Hebrew 8:12:

> "For I will forgive their wickedness and remember their sins no more."

And in 2 Corinthians 5:21, it is written:

> "God made Him who had no sin to be sin for us, so that in Him we might become the righteousness of God."

Many people do not know about the true Sabbath. And many of those who know do not keep it holy and are shy to tell others about it. Let us pray that through reading the Bible this message of God's Love will be made even clearer to all mankind. You and I are forgiven. By His wounds we are healed. What remains is for us to do our part—to seek the Lord with all our heart and all our mind and ask Him to lead us anew into the WHOLE BIBLE TRUTH!

As we conclude this chapter, here is an interesting way to look at the Ten Commandments.

- I was born to love the Lord my God
- I was not brought into this world to disobey His commands
- I was not brought into this world to have other gods
- I was not brought into this world to bow down to idols
- I was brought into this world to honor my father and mother
- I was not born into this world to lie
- I was not born into this world to covet what others have
- I was not born into this world to covet someone's wife
- God did not bring me into this world to steal from anyone

- He did not bring me into this world to hurt my brother, sister, mother, father or any neighbor
- He did not bring me into this world to be adulterous
- God did not bring me into this world to give false testimony
- And yes, He brought me into this world to observe and honor His declared Sabbath and keep it holy.

All who say that because Jesus came and because of the 'new covenant' the issues above are no longer relevant have been deceived. They are wrong. But the Lord still says, "Come to me, for you are my children." Forgiven children we are. Let us return to the Lord our God.

EPILOGUE

I recall vividly the day the call was made. I hadn't been in the frame of mind to absorb the shock I was about to receive. But within seconds of answering it, the news had been dropped on me without a preamble or preparation of any kind. The caller just went on to tell me that my son, Paul, had died in what was suspected to be suicide. I don't want to dwell on this matter except to say that later circumstantial evidence has proved just how far off such conclusions were. I'll let my son reveal his character posthumously in another book.

The reason I have opened this epilogue with the sudden demise of my son is because in his death, I came to realize that each of us has a reason why we have been placed in this world at any given point in time. I have gone through the writings he left behind—and listened to accounts of who he was from the lips of his friends—and come to the conclusion that in his short life, the boy had impacted more lives with his timely messages than many folks will ever do in a lifetime. He did so because he sensed his purpose for living early.

Unlike my son, it took me a little longer to get down to what the Lord wanted me to do. I have done many things right, though. I have worked in many countries, where I believe programs and other engagements I was part of have helped save and make the lives of many children better. I have also supported the interests of the poor, the orphans and widows in the region I come from by funding an NGO dedicated to the welfare of such needy folks. But even so, I have retained this restlessness that whatever the Lord wanted me to accomplish I have never really done.

It wasn't until I concluded writing this book that I finally felt the weight lifted. Let me explain. The weight was lifted because the message of the Sabbath was burning within me. Having come from a family of pioneer Adventist pastors—my paternal and maternal grandfathers were the first and second ordained Adventist pastors in the sub-Saharan Africa respectively—I have watched with dismay as successive generations of Adventists have treated the Sabbath with recklessness and even relegated its importance to that of any other day. I have burned with fear that if the prevalent tide of carelessness is not stemmed we may all completely lose sight of the importance of the day the Lord commanded His people to worship on.

But of even greater fear to me is the growing sense that any day of the week can be a day of rest. Haven't you heard arguments that we can count any seven days—starting from any day of the week—and make the seventh the day of rest? Worse still, have you not encountered the Evangelicals and Catholics who insist that the seventh day Sabbath no longer matters? The confusion such arguments cause in the minds of gullible people is enormous—and extremely destructive. And though the Lord will hold accountable the folks who mislead His flock, He will hold us just as accountable for failing to lead the flock back to the path of righteousness.

I believe that is why the Holy Spirit inspired the writing of this book.

What you have read in the pages of this volume is a way of telling people all over the world to trace back our roots to the creative week of *Genesis*. In spite of the devastation and calamities we have witnessed—and continue to witness—in this world, God intended a good life for man. That fact is not in doubt. And even though sin came in to cut that harmonious link that should have characterized man's relationship with God, the Creator made provision for the continued existence of a relationship even on this damaged side of eternity. That provision runs through recognition of Him as the creator and His son Jesus Christ as the redeemer.

I will continue to proclaim it on the mountains and down the valleys that there is rest only in a true understanding of what God meant when He said REMEMBER. God did not want to burden us with more things than we could deal with. Our feverish studying of the world around us, leading to the attainment of lofty degrees in disciplines that define life, was not His intended path for worship of Him; He just wanted us to remember that He created us. I guess His thinking was that anybody with common sense would observe the majesty of the Milky Way, the glory of the Andromeda and the rhythmic thumping of the heart for years, and automatically bow down in reverence and praise of such a wonderful creator. He expected the evidence of His majesty to speak for itself. But it didn't!

The task you and I have today is to remind the world that the God who created us also redeemed us. He has double ownership of us. The truth is—as things stand now, if Christ were to return today to bring those who have kept the fourth commandment home, He would end up with very few. A scornful world has turned its back on its creator. In the balance of time we have, before He returns to take His own home, we have the herculean task to stop the continued lies of the Catholics, the complicity of the Protestants who are now in bed with Catholicism on the Sabbath issue, and the complacency of those who keep the Sabbath that has eroded the significance of the Sabbath among our people. Can this be easy? No, it can't. But we have no alternative, because as Christ said in Mathew, just before He left for heaven, we have to go into all the world and preach the good news of His creation and redemption of mankind. We have to call the world back to a place called REMEMBER. That's why we are here!

www.ingramcontent.com/pod-product-compliance
Lightning Source LLC
Chambersburg PA
CBHW042322150426
43192CB00001B/17